# Sir Walter Ralegh

The Poems, with other Verse from the Court of Elizabeth I

Selected and edited by MARTIN DODSWORTH

Royal Holloway, University of London

EVERYMAN
J. M. Dent · London

This edition first published by Everyman Paperbacks in 1999
Selection, introduction and other critical apparatus
© J.M. Dent 1999

All rights reserved

J.M. Dent
Orion Publishing Group
Orion House
5 Upper Saint Martin's Lane
London WC2H 9EA

Typeset by Deltatype Ltd, Birkenhead, Merseyside
Printed in Great Britain by
The Guernsey Press Co. Ltd, Guernsey, C.I.

This book if bound as a paperback is subject to the condition
that it may not be issued on loan or otherwise except
in its original binding.

British Library Cataloguing-in-Publication
Data is available upon request

ISBN 0 460 87994 4

# Contents

*Note on the Author and Editor*  vii
*Chronology of Ralegh's Life and Times*  viii
*Introduction*  xvi

## I  The Poems of Sir Walter Ralegh

1. In Commendation of *The Steel Glass*  3
2. A Farewell to False Love  4
2a. 'Most welcome Love, thou mortal foe to lies' [a reply by Sir Thomas Heneage]  5
3. An Epitaph Upon the Right Honourable Sir Philip Sidney, Knight, Lord Governor of Flushing (died 1586)  6
4. 'Fortune hath taken thee away, my love'  8
4a. 'Ah, silly pug, wert thou so sore afraid?' [an answer by Queen Elizabeth I]  9
5. An Epigram on Henry Noel  10
5a. 'The foe to the stomach and the word of disgrace' [an answer by Henry Noel]  10
6. The Excuse  11
7. A Vision upon this Conceit of *The Faerie Queene*  12
8. Another of the Same  13
9. Farewell to the Court  14
10. 'Now we have present made'  15
11. 'If Cynthia be a queen, a princess and supreme'  16
12. 'My body in the walls captiv'd'  17
13. The One-and-twentieth and Last Book of the Ocean to Cynthia  18
14. The End of the Books of the Ocean's Love to Cynthia  33
15. The Lie  34

15a. 'Go, echo of the mind, a careless truth protest'
     [an answer, possibly by Robert Devereux, Earl of
     Essex]   37
16.  'Nature, that wash'd her hands in milk'   38
17.  'What is our life? It is a play of passion'   39
18.  To the Translator of Lucan   40
19.  A Petition to Queen Anne   41
20.  'My broken pipes shall on the willow hang'   44
21.  'Ev'n such is time, which takes in trust'   45
22.  Verse Translations from *The History of the World*   46

## II  Poems Sometimes Attributed to Sir Walter Ralegh

23. 'Sweet are the thoughts where Hope persuadeth Hap'  53
24. A Poem put into my Lady Leighton's Pocket  54
25. A Poesy to Prove Affection is not Love  55
26. 'Passions are liken'd best to floods and streams'  56
27. Sir Walter Ralegh to his Son  57
28. The Passionate Man's Pilgrimage  58
29. 'As you came from the holy land'  60
30a. The Passionate Shepherd to his Love [by Christopher Marlowe]  62
30. The Nymph's reply to the Shepherd  63
31. The Advice  64
32. 'Prais'd be Diana's fair and harmless light'  65
33. 'Like to a hermit poor in place obscure'  66
34. 'Feed still thyself, thou fondling, with belief'  67
35. 'My first-born love, unhappily conceiv'd'  68
36. 'Those eyes which set my fancy on a fire'  69
37. 'A secret murder hath been done of late'  70
38. 'Sought by the world, and hath the world disdain'd'  71
39. 'What else is hell but loss of blissful heaven?'  72
40. On the Cards and the Dice  73
41. Sir W. Ralegh on the Snuff of a Candle the Night before he Died  74

## III  Poems from the Court of Elizabeth I

### ELIZABETH I, QUEEN OF ENGLAND
42. 'A hapless kind of life is this I wear'   77
42a. 'Madam, but mark the labours of our life' [an answer by Sir Thomas Heneage]   77
43. 'The doubt of future foes exiles my present joy'   78
44. On Monsieur's Departure   79
45. 'Now leave and let me rest'   80

### ROBERT DEVEREUX, EARL OF ESSEX
46. 'Seated between the old world and the new'   82
47. 'Change thy mind since she doth change'   83
48. 'To plead my faith where faith hath no reward'   84
49. 'Happy were he could finish forth his fate'   85
50. Verses Made by the Earl of Essex in his Trouble   86
51. 'I am not as I seem, I seem and am the same'   87

### EDWARD DE VERE, EARL OF OXFORD
52. 'I am not as I seem to be'   88
53. 'The lively lark stretch'd forth her wing'   89
54. 'When wert thou born, Desire?'   90

### SIR THOMAS HENEAGE
55. 'Idle or else but seldom busied best'   91

### SIR HENRY LEE
56. Sir Henry Lee's Farewell to the Court   92
57. 'Time's eldest son, Old Age, the heir of Ease'   93
58. 'Far from triumphing court and wonted glory'   94

*Notes*   95
*Index of First Lines*   104
*Acknowledgements*   106

# Note on the Author and Editor

SIR WALTER RALEGH was born in 1554, the child of Devon gentry with sea-going connections. He studied at Oxford and the Inns of Court and by 1580 was on military service in Ireland, where he met the poet Edmund Spenser. His knowledge of Irish affairs brought him to the attention of Elizabeth I and from 1582 he rose steadily at court, being knighted in 1585, the same year in which he attempted to establish the first English colony in America. He fought against the Spanish Armada and in various naval expeditions. In 1592 his secret marriage to Elizabeth Throckmorton led to loss of the Queen's favour and a brief imprisonment in the Tower of London. By 1595 he had to some extent regained royal favour, but experienced a sudden and decisive reversal in 1603 when Elizabeth died and was replaced by the Scottish king, James. Ralegh was quickly charged with treason, sentenced to death, had the sentence commuted and spent the next thirteen years a prisoner in the Tower of London. Here he wrote his *History of the World* (1614), which displeased the King and was suppressed by him. At last, in 1616 and at the age of 62, Ralegh persuaded the King to release him in order to undertake a voyage to 'Guiana', where he believed there was gold to be found. The expedition was a disaster. Ralegh obstinately returned to England and was once again sentenced to death. He was beheaded in 1618.

MARTIN DODSWORTH is Professor of English at Royal Holloway, University of London. He is editor of the Everyman Poetry *Shakespeare*, and author of *Hamlet Closely Observed* (1985). He worked for many years on the Oxford edition of Burton's *Anatomy of Melancholy* and for ten years edited the journal *English*.

# Chronology of Ralegh's Life

| Year | Age | Life |
|---|---|---|
| 1554 | | Born at Hayes, Devon, his father's youngest son by his second wife, herself the mother of two older boys by a previous marriage |
| 1572 | 18 | At Oriel College, Oxford, where he probably spent three years in all |
| 1575 | 21 | At the Inns of Court, London, transferring from Lyon's Inn to the Middle Temple |
| 1576 | 22 | First appearance in print: the commendatory poem for *The Steel Glass* by George Gascoigne, a friend of his half-brother, Sir Humphrey Gilbert |
| 1578 | 24 | Captains a ship in Gilbert's unsuccessful attempt to discover the Northwest Passage to China |
| 1580 | 26 | Military service in Ireland under the Lord Deputy, Lord Gray. Present at the slaughterous siege of Smerwick and returns to London with papers retrieved there |

# Chronology of his Times

| Year | Artistic Events | Historical Events |
|------|-----------------|-------------------|
| 1554 | | Queen Mary of England marries Philip of Spain |
| 1557 | *Tottel's Miscellany* (*Songs and Sonnets*) by Wyatt, Surrey *et al* | |
| 1558 | | Death of Mary; accession of Elizabeth I |
| 1559 | *Mirror for Magistrates* | |
| 1560 | Geneva Bible is published | |
| 1561 | Hoby's translation of Castiglione's *The Courtier* | |
| 1569 | | Northern Rebellion crushed |
| 1570 | Ascham, *The Schoolmaster* | Elizabeth excommunicated |
| 1576 | Building of the first playhouse in London | |
| 1577 | Sidney, 'Old' *Arcadia* begun | Drake starts voyage round world |
| 1578 | Lyly, *Euphues* | |
| 1579 | Spenser, *The Shepheardes Calender* | |

| Year | Age | Life |
|------|-----|------|
| 1581 | 27 | Returns briefly to Ireland; probable first meeting with Edmund Spenser. Back in London by end of year |
| 1582 | 28 | In favour with Elizabeth I; accompanies the Duke of Anjou on his return to Antwerp |
| 1583 | 29 | Granted profitable patent to license retailers of wine |
| 1584 | 30 | Granted patent to seek new lands, and sponsors first voyage to America; also given a patent for broadcloth export. Sits in his first Parliament |
| 1585 | 31 | Knighted by Elizabeth. First attempt to establish colony in 'Virginia' (North Carolina). Appointed Steward of the Duchy of Cornwall and Warden of the Stannaries (Cornish tin mines) |
| 1586 | 32 | Grant of considerable lands in Ireland. Member of Parliament again. Becomes Captain of the Queen's Guard about this time |
| 1587 | 33 | Lord Lieutenant of Cornwall; still occupied with colonization project for 'Virginia' |
| 1588 | 34 | Marries Elizabeth Throckmorton without the Queen's knowledge. Serves in the English Channel against the Spanish Armada |
| 1589 | 35 | Withdraws from the Virginia colony project. Visits Ireland briefly, meets with Spenser and brings him to court at end of year |
| 1591 | 37 | Charged with responsibility of defence against Spanish attack. His kinsman, Sir Richard Grenville, dies on the *Revenge* in battle against the Spaniards and is commemorated in a tract on the encounter by Ralegh |
| 1592 | 38 | Elizabeth learns of Ralegh's marriage, summons him back from a privateering expedition and puts both him and his wife in the Tower of London for a couple of months |
| 1593 | 39 | Serves once more as Member of Parliament. Birth of his son Walter |

| Year | Artistic Events | Historical Events |
|---|---|---|
| 1585 | | Leicester leads expedition to Netherlands |
| 1586 | | Sidney dies at Zutphen |
| 1587 | | Mary Queen of Scots executed<br>Drake at Cadiz |
| 1588 | Shakespeare's earliest plays performed | Defeat of Spanish Armada |
| 1589 | Hakluyt, *Principal Navigations* | |
| 1590 | Marlowe, *Tamburlaine*<br>Sidney, 'New' *Arcadia*<br>Spenser, *Faerie Queene*, i–iii | |
| 1591 | Sidney, *Astrophil and Stella* | |
| 1593 | Shakespeare, *Venus and Adonis* | |

| Year | Age | Life |
|---|---|---|
| 1594 | 40 | Elizabeth authorizes his continuing ventures against Spain |
| 1595 | 41 | Voyage to 'Guiana' – the Orinoco basin |
| 1596 | 42 | Publishes *The Discovery . . . of Guiana*; with Essex in storming of Cadiz |
| 1597 | 43 | Resumes his duties as Captain of the Guard; takes part in unsuccessful raiding voyage to the Azores; seizes the island of Fayal |
| 1598 | 44 | Member of Parliament again |
| 1600 | 46 | Made Governor of Jersey |
| 1601 | 47 | Sits (for last time) in Parliament |
| 1603 | 49 | Loses his patents and offices on accession of James. Convicted of high treason on no evidence; death sentence commuted to imprisonment |
| 1603– 1616 | 49– 62 | A prisoner in the Tower of London, occupied in chemical and pharmacological experiments, in writing and in a successful campaign to win favour with James's consort, Anne of Denmark, and their eldest son, Prince Henry |
| 1614 | 60 | Ralegh's *History of the World* published and suppressed by James |

| Year | Artistic Events | Historical Events |
|---|---|---|
| 1594 | Shakespeare, *Lucrece* | |
| 1595 | Spenser, *Amoretti* | Drake and Hawkins die in unsuccessful West Indies voyage |
| 1596 | Sidney, *Apology for Poetry*<br>Spenser, *Faerie Queene*, iv–vi | Spanish capture Calais |
| 1597 | Bacon, *Essays* | |
| 1598 | Marlowe, *Hero and Leander* | Rebellion in Ireland<br>Philip of Spain dies |
| 1599 | | Essex fails as Lord Deputy in Ireland; returns, is imprisoned |
| 1600 | Shakespeare, *Hamlet* acted | East India Company founded |
| 1601 | | Essex rebels and is executed |
| 1603 | | Death of Elizabeth I; accession of James I |
| 1604 | | Peace with Spain |
| 1605 | Bacon, *Advancement of Learning* | Gunpowder Plot defeated |
| 1607 | | English colony established in Virginia |
| 1608 | Shakespeare, *Coriolanus* acted | |
| 1609 | | Oath of Allegiance<br>Truce in Netherlands |
| 1611 | Authorized Version of the Bible | |
| 1612 | | Death of Prince Henry |
| 1613 | | Marriage of Princess Elizabeth to Elector Palatine |

| Year | Age | Life |
|------|-----|------|
| 1616 | 62 | Released from the Tower to prepare for an expedition to Guiana |
| 1617 | 63 | The Guiana voyage proves disastrous. Ralegh loses his son Walter |
| 1618 | 64 | On his return home, put under arrest. Attempts escape to France. The death sentence of 1603 is revived. Executed 29 October |

| Year | Artistic Events | Historical Events |
|------|-----------------|-------------------|
| 1616 | Jonson, *Works* | |

All dates for books and plays are those of publication unless otherwise stated.

# Introduction

In his *Worthies of England* the seventeenth-century writer Thomas Fuller tells several stories about Sir Walter Ralegh. One of them is the famous tale of his winning favour by spreading his cloak over a puddle that stood in the way of the Queen as she walked out. Another far more plausible story has Ralegh at court, uncertain as to his prospects of rising there, writing with a diamond on a window where Elizabeth would see it the single line 'Fain would I climb, yet fear I to fall'. According to Fuller, the Queen coming across it wrote underneath: 'If thy heart fails thee, climb not at all'. The put-down, tough and challenging at the same time, seems fully characteristic of the remarkable woman who ruled England and a court full of ambitious men with equal success for more than forty years. That it should be in verse says something about the way in which she ruled that court, imposing a standard of 'civilized' conduct on men whose passions were often violent and just as frequently self-centred. But of course it is the frankness with which Ralegh announces his desire to 'climb' that is most striking; it hits off the man and his environment to perfection. It was a hard and ruthless world, for all its veneer of civilization. It is hard not to think of Donne's satire 'The Progress of the Soul':

>     Fish chaseth fish, and all,
> Flyer and follower, in this whirlpool fall;
> O might not states of more equality
> Consist? and is it of necessity
> That thousand guiltless smalls, to make one great, must die?

Ralegh, we can be sure, did not intend to be one of the 'smalls' who would die. He was an adventurer and always gambled for high stakes. In one sense, he had to. He was a younger son of a respectable gentry family which could not put great means at his disposal. If he was to succeed he could rely on himself alone. And he did succeed. He won the Queen's favour, lost it and regained it. At his height, he was a very rich man. He owned thousands of acres in

Ireland, drew a good income from the various offices the Queen gave him, lived in a fine London house which she had leased to him. He invested heavily in voyages of discovery and privateering (the two were not easy to distinguish) and went to sea himself when Elizabeth permitted it. He set up the first colony in North America; it failed, but the dream of wealth stayed with him and when he died it was as the result of another attempt to make money from colonization, this time in 'Guiana', the basin of the Orinoco in present-day Venezuela which he had first visited in 1595.

He was a man of action, but not only that. He was a courtier and a parliamentarian, a poet and a thinker. His philosophy was tried by two spells in the Tower of London, the second one lasting for more than twelve years, during which he wrote an enormous *History of the World* besides other tracts, at the same time conducting experiments in chemistry and pharmacology. His first imprisonment there had been the result of his secret marriage to Elizabeth Throckmorton, a marriage which had enraged the Queen and brought him close to destruction. The tenderness which he displayed in his letters to his wife and children thereafter is another important facet of this many-sided man. If he was an adventurer, he was not just an adventurer.

But he was a climber, and poetry was one of the means by which he climbed. It was not enough for a courtier simply to be present at court. A man had to distinguish himself by his conduct and part of his distinction should be his skill in writing. In 1561, three years after Elizabeth had come to the throne, Sir Thomas Hoby published his translation of *The Courtier* by the Italian Baldassare Castiglione; this book set forth an ideal to which the hopeful courtier might aspire. 'Let him much exercise himself in poets, and no less in orators and historiographers, and also in writing both rhyme and prose, and especially in this our vulgar tongue.' Like Sir Philip Sidney, for whom he wrote an elegy, Ralegh took this advice to heart. The poems printed alongside his own in this volume suggest that, from a prudential point of view, he was right to do so. The rivalries of court expressed themselves, not exclusively but to a significant degree, in the verses courtiers wrote seeking the Queen's favour. If answers survive to more than one of Ralegh's poems, that is because in the game of courting Elizabeth's favour they were important, and the game was more than a game. That Elizabeth herself should have written a poem in reply to one of Ralegh's was a sign of exceptional favour; it was an act of power as much as, or even more than, a graceful literary exercise. The fact that many of the poems of Elizabeth's courtiers trade in the familiar imagery of the Petrarchan love poem – hearts on fire, eyes that pierce, love that endures – should not blind us to the kind of favour that, beneath all this, was being sought: an estate in Northamptonshire, perhaps, or membership of the Privy Council (something Ralegh never achieved).

Poetry was important as a means to an end, not in itself. That would seem to be what is implied by Ralegh's poetry. The very difficulty we have in identifying which poems are his testifies to the author's indifference to their fate once they had gained their end. It was, in any case, bad form to make too much of any gift; Castiglione's courtier was 'to seem not to mind the thing a man doth excellently well'. So Sir Philip Sidney's poems went unpublished in his lifetime, as did Ralegh's, with the exception of his commendatory poems for others. Ascriptions to him in manuscripts are notoriously unreliable, partly because his posthumous celebrity as a victim of the unreasonable wrath of James I attracted all kinds of rebellious and courtly poems to his name, partly because he never took care of his own manuscripts in his lifetime.

It might seem from all this that Ralegh's poetry must be devoid of poetic interest, that it could not be anything other than a collection of frigid conceits. And yet this is not the case. Ralegh's poetry is forceful and convincing, frequently suggesting that where his ambition was his love lay also. 'The Ocean's Love to Cynthia' is a good example. It was probably written at the time of the poet's disgrace over his marriage, as an attempt to persuade the Queen that she was the woman Ralegh truly loved, however much the facts might seem against him. It must seem implausible that it should succeed, and yet it does:

> So, in the centre of my cloven heart,
> My heart, to whom her beauties were such wonder,
> Lies the sharp poison'd head of that love's dart,
>
> Which, till all break and all dissolve to dust,
> Thence drawn it cannot be, or therein known.

The power of this verse lies partly in its emphases, the repetitions of 'heart' and 'all', the clotted stresses of '*sharp pois*on'd *dart*', partly in its runs of the briefest, hence most truthful, words – 'Which, till all break and all . . .' – partly in the very commonplace nature of its imagery which, by 'wonder', 'dart' and 'dust', suggests that the experience described is universal, does not need far-fetched similes to describe its disastrous totality. Whatever the means, this is a poetry that completely answers the test of feeling. 'She is gone, she is lost! she is found, she is ever fair!' There is something naked about this paradoxical assertion, something unformalized, unconventional, as we may discover if we compare it with, say, 'thou met'st with things dying, I with things new-born' from *The Winter's Tale* or Pericles' cry to his new-found daughter – 'Thou that beget'st him that did thee beget'. This naked quality in 'The Ocean's Love to Cynthia' is enhanced by the poem's incompleteness, its false starts, its peterings-out, which may be products of art after all, rather than the marks of work in progress.

It is not just that Ralegh feels strongly about the Queen. He feels anguish at his own situation and the terrible impermanency that belongs to it. His end, executed at the whim of a monarch after the ruination of his dreams, justified the anguish; the anguish, in which we can all share, justifies the poems. That is why 'The Lie' belongs in the canon of Ralegh's poems. Scholars feel that it is not quite good enough for Ralegh; what they mean is that the artful artlessness of this poem goes too viciously deep.

> Say to the Court, it glows
> And shines like rotten wood . . .

The paradox of glow and shine linked to rot is central to 'The Ocean's Love to Cynthia' as it is to 'Nature, that wash'd her hands in milk' or, in a different way, 'What is our life? It is a play of passion'.

Ralegh recognized early the significance of Spenser's poetry, and wrote two commendatory poems for the first instalment of *The Faerie Queene* besides introducing Spenser to court. The first of the two commendatory poems is an acknowledged masterpiece which ends with 'groans of buried ghosts . . .'

> Where Homer's sprite did tremble all for grief,
> And curs'd th'access of that celestial thief.

Celebration, for Ralegh, entails a knowledge of harm elsewhere, and the poem's jubilant music is based on groans and thievery. The association of Ralegh and Spenser is no accident; both share a vision of the world's wonders as ready to tumble at a moment's notice. Spenser's court of Lucifera conceals a dungeon 'Of caitiff wretched thralls, that wailed night and day':

> There was that great proud king of Babylon
> That would compel all nations to adore
> And him as only god to call upon,
> Till through celestial doom thrown out of door
> Into an ox he was transform'd of yore . . .

This is the same perilous court which Ralegh's poems inhabit. But the difference between Spenser and Ralegh lies in the much more pointed nature of the latter's poems; they feel more acutely.

A tacit acknowledgement of the principle of anguish at work in Ralegh's poems is the attribution to him of two poems 'written the night before he died'. It is as though his poems were inevitably written on the point of death. The unlikely attribution to him of the famous 'The Passionate Man's Pilgrimage' is probably part of this tradition; it is, after all, a poem supposed to be spoken or written by a man about to be beheaded, as Ralegh was. The simplicity of its faith, its 'nectar suckets' and 'crystal buckets' do not seem much like what we know of his other poems, but there is a downrightness to it that can be paralleled elsewhere in his work; 'Farewell, false Love, thou oracle of lies', 'Like truthless dreams, so are my joys expir'd' – this facing-up to unpalatable truths might be based on an enabling faith even if it appears little elsewhere. But really it is the steeliness of Ralegh's verse that prevails over any simplicity, the fixity of the mind that seizes 'The grief remaining of the joy it had'.

This quality is reflected also in Ralegh's tendency to use lines of his own verse in later compositions, as happens with 'Farewell to the Court' and 'The Ocean's Love' or the 'last book' of 'The Ocean's Love' and the 'Petition to Queen Anne'. It is a way of standing by the written word, as though to say the poems exceed their occasions; in writing for ambition, Ralegh also wrote himself into being, a self ever aware of the dungeon beneath Lucifera's court or the Tower where he eventually found himself.

> Stab at thee he that will,
> No stab the soul can kill.

MARTIN DODSWORTH

# I

# The Poems of Sir Walter Ralegh

## 1. **In Commendation of** *The Steel Glass*

Sweet were the sauce would please each kind of taste;
The life likewise were pure that never swerv'd:
For spiteful tongues in canker'd stomachs plac'd
Deem worst of things which best (percase) deserv'd.
But what for that? This medicine may suffice 5
To scorn the rest, and seek to please the wise.

Though sundry minds in sundry sort do deem,
Yet worthiest wights yield praise for every pain;
But envious brains do nought, or light, esteem
Such stately steps as they cannot attain. 10
For whoso reaps renown above the rest,
With heaps of hate shall surely be oppress'd.

Wherefore, to write my censure of this book,
This Glass of Steel unpartially doth show
Abuses all to such as in it look, 15
From prince to poor, from high estate to low.
As for the verse, who list like trade to try,
I fear me much, shall hardly reach so high.

## 2. A Farewell to False Love

Farewell, false Love, thou oracle of lies,
A mortal foe, an enemy to rest,
An envious boy from whom all cares arise,
A bastard born, a beast with rage possess'd,
A way of error, a temple full of treason,
In all effects contrary unto reason;

A poison'd serpent, cover'd all with flowers,
Mother of sighs and murderer of repose,
A sea of sorrows, from whence are drawn such showers
As moisture lends to ev'ry grief that grows;
A school of guile, a nest of deep deceit,
A gilded hook that holds a poison'd bait;

A fortress foil'd whom reason did defend,
A siren song, a fever of the mind,
A maze wherein affection finds no end,
A ranging cloud that runs before the wind,
A substance like the shadow of the sun,
A goal of grief for which the wisest run.

## 2a. 'Most welcome Love, thou mortal foe to lies'

[a reply by Sir Thomas Heneage]

Most welcome Love, thou mortal foe to lies,
Thou root of life and ruiner of debate,
An imp of heaven, that troth to virtue ties,
A sun of choice, that bastard lusts doth hate;
A way to fasten fancy most to reason
In all effects, and enemy most to treason;

A flower of faith, that will not fade for smart,
Mother of trust and murderer of our woes,
In Sorrow's sea a cordial to the heart
That med'cine gives to ev'ry grief that grows;
A school of wit, a nest of sweet conceit,
A piercing eye that finds a gilt deceit;

A fortress sure which reason must defend,
A hopeful toil, a most delighting band,
Affection maz'd, that leads to happy end;
To ranging thoughts a gentle reining hand;
A substance such as will not be undone,
A prize of joy for which the wisest run.

# 3. An Epitaph Upon the Right Honourable Sir Philip Sidney, Knight, Lord Governor of Flushing (died 1586)

To praise thy life or wail thy worthy death
And want thy wit, thy wit high, pure, divine,
Is far beyond the power of mortal line,
Nor any one hath worth that draweth breath;

Yet rich in zeal, though poor in learning's lore,                5
And friendly care, obscur'd in secret breast,
And love, that envy in thy life suppress'd,
Thy dear life done, thy death hath doubled more,

And I, that in thy time and living state
Did only praise thy virtues in my thought,                       10
As one that seld the rising sun hath sought,
With words and tears now wail thy timeless fate.

Drawn was thy race aright from princely line;
Nor less than such, by gifts that nature gave,
The common mother that all creatures have,                       15
Doth virtue show, and princely lineage shine.

A king gave thee thy name; a kingly mind,
That God thee gave, who found it now too dear
For this base world, and hath resum'd it near
To sit in skies, and sort with powers divine.                    20

Kent thy birth-days, and Oxford held thy youth;
The heavens made haste, and stayed nor years nor time;
The fruits of age grew ripe in thy first prime;
Thy will, thy words; thy words the seals of truth.

Great gifts and wisdom rare employ'd thee thence,                25
To treat from kings with those more great than kings;
Such hope men had to lay the highest things
On thy wise youth, to be transported hence.

Whence to sharp wars sweet honour did thee call,
Thy country's love, religion, and thy friends      30
(Of worthy men the marks, the lives, and ends)
And her defence, for whom we labour all.

There didst thou vanquish shame and tedious age,
Grief, sorrow, sickness, and base fortune's might;
Thy rising day saw never woeful night,      35
But pass'd with praise from off this worldly stage.

Back to the camp by thee that day was brought,
First, thine own death, and after, thy long fame;
Tears to the soldiers; the proud Castilians shame;
Virtue express'd, and honour truly taught.      40

What hath he lost that such great grace hath won?
Young years for endless years, and hope unsure
Of fortune's gifts for wealth that still shall dure:
O happy race, with so great praises run!

England doth hold thy limbs, that bred the same;      45
Flanders thy valour, where it last was tried;
The camp thy sorrow, where thy body died;
Thy friends thy want; the world thy virtue's fame;

Nations thy wit. Our minds lay up thy love;
Letters thy learning; thy loss long years to come.      50
In worthy hearts sorrow hath made thy tomb;
Thy soul and sprite enrich the heavens above.

The lib'ral heart embalm'd in grateful tears,
Young sighs, sweet sighs, sage sighs, bewail thy fall;
Envy her sting, and spite hath left her gall;      55
Malice herself a mourning garment wears.

That day their Hannibal died, our Scipio fell, –
Scipio, Cicero, and Petrarch of our time;
Whose virtues, wounded by my worthless rhyme,
Let angels speak, and heaven thy praises tell.

## 4. 'Fortune hath taken thee away, my love'

Fortune hath taken thee away, my love,
My life's joy and my soul's heaven above;
Fortune hath taken thee away, my princess,
My world's delight and my true fancy's mistress.

Fortune hath taken all away from me, 5
Fortune hath taken all by taking thee;
Dead to all joys, I only live to woe,
So Fortune now becomes my fancy's foe.

In vain, mine eyes, in vain you waste your tears;
In vain, my sighs, the smokes of my despairs, 10
In vain you search the earth and heavens above,
In vain you search, for Fortune keeps my love.

Then will I leave my love in Fortune's hands,
Then will I leave my love in worthless bands,
And only love the sorrow due to me, 15
Sorrow henceforth that shall my princess be,

And only joy that Fortune conquers kings.
Fortune that rules on earth and earthly things
Hath ta'en my love in spite of virtue's might.
So blind a goddess did never virtue right. 20

With Wisdom's eyes had but blind Fortune seen,
Then had my love my love for ever been;
But Love, farewell; though Fortune conquer thee,
No fortune base shall ever alter me.

## 4a. 'Ah, silly pug, wert thou so sore afraid?'

[an answer by Queen Elizabeth I]

Ah, silly pug, wert thou so sore afraid?
Mourn not, my Wat, nor be thou so dismay'd;
It passeth fickle Fortune's power and skill
To force my heart to think thee any ill.

No fortune base, thou sayst, shall alter thee;  5
And may so blind a wretch then conquer me?
No, no, my pug, though Fortune were not blind,
Assure thyself she could not rule my mind.

Ne choose I thee by foolish Fortune's rede,
Ne can she make me alter with such speed;  10
But must thou needs sour Sorrow's servant be,
If that to try thy mistress jest with thee.

Fortune, I grant, doth sometimes conquer kings,
And rules and reigns on earth and earthly things,
But never think that Fortune can bear sway  15
If Virtue watch and will her not obey.

Pluck up thy heart, suppress thy brackish tears,
Torment thee not, but put away thy fears;
Thy love, thy joy – she loves no worthless bands,
Much less to be in reeling Fortune's hands.  20

Dead to all joys and living unto woe,
Slain quite by her that never gave wise man blow,
Revive again and live without all dread.
The less afraid, the better thou shalt speed.

## 5. An Epigram on Henry Noel

The word of denial and the letter of fifty
Makes the gentleman's name that will never be thrifty.

## 5a. 'The foe to the stomach and the word of disgrace'

[an answer by Henry Noel]

The foe to the stomach and the word of disgrace
Shows the gentleman's name with the bold face.

## 6. The Excuse

Calling to mind mine eye went long about
To cause my heart for to forsake my breast,
All in a rage I thought to pull it out,
By whose device I liv'd in such unrest.
What could it say then to regain my grace? –
Forsooth, that it had seen my mistress' face.

Another time, I called unto mind,
It was my heart which all this woe had wrought,
Because that he to Love his fort resign'd,
When on such wars my fancy never thought.
What could he say when I would him have slain? –
That he was yours, and had forgone me clean.

At length, when I perceiv'd both eye and heart
Excuse themselves, as guiltless of mine ill,
I found myself the cause of all my smart,
And told myself, 'Myself now slay I will.'
Yet when I saw myself to you was true,
I lov'd myself, because myself lov'd you.

# 7. A Vision upon this Conceit of *The Faerie Queene*

Methought I saw the grave where Laura lay
Within that temple where the vestal flame
Was wont to burn: and, passing by that way,
To see that buried dust of living fame,
Whose tomb fair Love and fairer Virtue kept,   5
All suddenly I saw the Fairy Queen,
At whose approach the soul of Petrarch wept;
And from thenceforth those graces were not seen,
For they this Queen attended; in whose stead
Oblivion laid him down on Laura's hearse.   10
Hereat the hardest stones were seen to bleed,
And groans of buried ghosts the heavens did pierce:
    Where Homer's sprite did tremble all for grief,
    And curs'd th'access of that celestial thief.

## 8. Another of the Same

The praise of meaner wits this work like profit brings
As doth the cuckoo's song delight when Philumena sings.
If thou hast formed right true virtue's face herein,
Virtue herself can best discern, to whom they written been.
If thou hast beauty prais'd, let her sole looks divine 5
Judge if aught therein be amiss, and mend it by her eyne.
If Chastity want aught, or Temperance her due,
Behold her princely mind aright, and write thy Queen anew.
Meanwhile she shall perceive how far her virtues soar
Above the reach of all that live, or such as wrote of yore: 10
And thereby will excuse and favour thy good will,
Whose virtue cannot be express'd but by an angel's quill.
    Of me no lines are lov'd nor letters are of price,
      Of all which speak our English tongue, but those of thy
        device.

## 9. Farewell to the Court

Like truthless dreams, so are my joys expir'd,
And past return are all my dandled days,
My love misled, and fancy quite retir'd;
Of all which past, the sorrow only stays.

My lost delights, now clean from sight of land,
Have left me all alone in unknown ways,
My mind to woe, my life in fortune's hand;
Of all which past, the sorrow only stays.

As in a country strange without companion,
I only wail the wrong of death's delays,
Whose sweet spring spent, whose summer well nigh done;
Of all which past, the sorrow only stays;

Whom care forewarns, ere age and winter cold,
To haste me hence to find my fortune's fold.

## 10. 'Now we have present made'

Now we have present made
To Cynthia, Phoebe, Flora,
Diana and Aurora,
Beauty that cannot fade,

A flower of Love's own planting,
A pattern kept by Nature
For beauty, form and stature
When she would frame a darling.

She is the valley of Peru
Whose summer ever lasteth.
Time conqu'ring all she mast'reth
By being alway new.

As elemental fire
Whose food and flame consumes not,
Or as the passion ends not
Of virtue's true desire,

So her celestial frame
And quintessential mind,
Which heavens together bind,
Shall ever be the same.

Then to her servants leave her,
Love, Nature and Affection,
Princess of world's perfection.
Our praises but deceive her.

If Love could find a quill
Drawn from an angel's wing,
Or did the Muses sing
That pretty wanton's will,

Perchance he could indict
To please all other sense;
But love's and woe's expense
Sorrow can only write.

## 11. 'If Cynthia be a queen, a princess and supreme'

If Cynthia be a queen, a princess and supreme,
Keep these among the rest, or say it was a dream;
For those that like, expound, and those that loathe, express
Meanings according as their minds are moved more or less.
For writing what thou art, or showing what thou were,     5
Adds to the one disdain, to the other but despair.
Thy mind of neither needs, in both seeing it exceeds.

## 12. 'My body in the walls captiv'd'

My body in the walls captiv'd
Feels not the wounds of spiteful envy;
But my thrall'd mind, of liberty depriv'd,
Fast fetter'd in her ancient memory,
Doth nought behold but sorrow's dying face.　　　　5
Such prison erst was so delightful,
As it desir'd no other dwelling place:
But time's effects and destinies despiteful
Have changed both my keeper and my fare.
Love's fire and beauty's light I then had store;　　　　10
But now, close kept, as captives wonted are,
That food, that heat, that light, I find no more.
    Despair bolts up my doors; and I alone
    Speak to dead walls; but those hear not my moan.

## 13. The One-and-twentieth and Last Book of the Ocean to Cynthia

Sufficeth it to you, my joys interr'd,
In simple words that I my woes complain;
You that then died when first my fancy err'd,
Joys under dust that never live again.

If to the living were my muse address'd,
Or did my mind her own spirit still inhold,
Were not my living passion so repress'd
As to the dead the dead did these unfold,

Some sweeter words, some more becoming verse
Should witness my mishap in higher kind;
But my love's wounds, my fancy in the hearse,
Th'idea but resting of a wasted mind,

The blossoms fall'n, the sap gone from the tree,
The broken monuments of my great desires,
From these so lost what may th'affections be?
What heat in cinders of extinguish'd fires?

Lost in the mud of those high-flowing streams,
Which through more fairer fields their courses bend,
Slain with self-thoughts, amaz'd in fearful dreams,
Woes without date, discomforts without end:

From fruitful trees I gather wither'd leaves,
And glean the broken ears with miser's hand,
Who sometime did enjoy the weighty sheaves;
I seek fair flowers amid the brinish sand.

All in the shade, even in the fair sun days,
Under those healthless trees I sit alone,
Where joyful birds sing neither lovely lays,
Nor Philomen recounts her direful moan.

No feeding flocks, no shepherd's company,
That might renew my dolorous conceit,
While happy then, while love and fantasy
Confin'd my thoughts on that fair flock to wait;

No pleasing streams fast to the ocean wending,
The messengers sometimes of my great woe;
But all on earth, as from the cold storms bending,
Shrink from my thoughts in high heavens or below.

O hopeful love, my object and invention,
O true desire, the spur of my conceit,
O worthiest spirit, my mind's impulsion,
O eyes transpersant, my affection's bait,

Oh, princely form, my fancy's adamant,
Divine conceit, my pains' acceptance,
O all in one! O heaven on earth transparent!
The seat of joys and love's abundance!

Out of that mass of miracles, my muse
Gather'd those flowers, to her pure senses pleasing;
Out of her eyes, the store of joys, did choose
Equal delights, my sorrows counterpoising.

Her regal looks my vigorous sighs suppress'd;
Small drops of joys sweeten'd great worlds of woes;
One gladsome day a thousand cares redress'd;
Whom love defends, what fortune overthrows?

When she did well, what did there else amiss?
When she did ill, what empires would have pleas'd?
No other power effecting woe or bliss,
She gave, she took, she wounded, she appeas'd.

The honour of her love Love still devising,
Wounding my mind with contrary conceit,
Transferred itself sometime to her aspiring,
Sometime the trumpet of her thought's retreat.

To seek new worlds for gold, for praise, for glory,
To try desire, to try love sever'd far,
When I was gone, she sent her memory,
More strong than were ten thousand ships of war,

To call me back, to leave great honour's thought,
To leave my friends, my fortune, my attempt;
To leave the purpose I so long had sought,
And hold both cares and comforts in contempt.

Such heat in ice, such fire in frost remain'd,
Such trust in doubt, such comfort in despair, 70
Much like the gentle lamb, though lately wean'd,
Plays with the dug, though finds no comfort there.

But as a body, violently slain,
Retaineth warmth although the spirit be gone,
And by a power in nature moves again 75
Till it be laid below the fatal stone;

Or as the earth, ev'n in cold winter days,
Left for a time by her life-giving sun,
Doth by the power remaining of his rays
Produce some green, though not as it hath done; 80

Or as a wheel, forc'd by the falling stream,
Although the course be turn'd some other way,
Doth for a time go round upon the beam,
Till, wanting strength to move, it stands at stay;

So my forsaken heart, my wither'd mind, 85
Widow of all the joys it once possess'd,
My hopes clean out of sight with forced wind,
To kingdoms strange, to lands far-off address'd,

Alone, forsaken, friendless, on the shore
With many wounds, with death's cold pangs embrac'd, 90
Writes in the dust, as one that could no more,
Whom love, and time, and fortune, had defac'd,

Of things so great, so long, so manifold,
With means so weak, the soul even then departing,
The weal, the woe, the passages of old, 95
And worlds of thoughts describ'd by one last sighing,

As if, when after Phoebus is descended,
And leaves a light much like the past day's dawning,
And, every toil and labour wholly ended,
Each living creature draweth to his resting, 100

We should begin by such a parting light
To write the story of all ages past,
And end the same before the approaching night.

Such is again the labour of my mind,
Whose shroud, by sorrow woven now to end,
Hath seen that ever shining sun declin'd,
So many years that so could not descend,

But that the eyes of my mind held her beams
In every part transferr'd by love's swift thought
Far off or near, in waking or in dreams;
Imagination strong their lustre brought,

Such force her angelic appearance had
To master distance, time, or cruelty;
Such art to grieve, and after to make glad;
Such fear in love, such love in majesty.

My weary limbs her memory embalm'd;
My darkest ways her eyes make clear as day.
What storms so great but Cynthia's beams appeas'd?
What rage so fierce that love could not allay?

Twelve years entire I wasted in this war,
Twelve years of my most happy younger days;
But I in them, and they now wasted are,
'Of all which past, the sorrow only stays.'

So wrate I once, and my mishap foretold,
My mind still feeling sorrowful success,
Ev'n as before a storm the marble cold
Doth by moist tears tempestuous times express.

So felt my heavy mind my harms at hand,
Which my vain thought in vain sought to recure:
At middle day my sun seem'd under land,
When any little cloud did it obscure.

And as the icicles in a winter's day,
Whenas the sun shines with unwonted warm,

So did my joys melt into secret tears;
So did my heart dissolve in wasting drops:
And as the season of the year outwears,
And heaps of snow from off the mountain tops

With sudden streams the valleys overflow,
So did the time draw on my more despair:

Then floods of sorrow and whole seas of woe
The banks of all my hope did overbear,

And drown'd my mind in depths of misery.
Sometime I died; sometime I was distract,
My soul the stage of fancy's tragedy;
Then furious madness, where true reason lack'd,

Wrate what it would, and scourg'd mine own conceit.
O heavy heart! who can thee witness bear?
What tongue, what pen, could thy tormenting treat,
But thine own mourning thoughts which present were?

What stranger mind believe the meanest part?
What alter'd sense conceive the weakest woe,
That tare, that rent, that pierced thy sad heart?

And as a man distract, with treble might,
Bound in strong chains, doth strive and rage in vain,
Till, tir'd and breathless, he is forc'd to rest,
Finds by contention but increase of pain,
And fiery heat inflam'd in swollen breast;

So did my mind in change of passion
From woe to wrath, from wrath return to woe,
Struggling in vain from love's subjection.

Therefore, all lifeless and all helpless bound,
My fainting spirits sunk, and heart apal'd,
My joys and hopes lay bleeding on the ground,
That not long since the highest heaven scal'd.

I hated life and cursed destiny;
The thoughts of passed times, like flames of hell,
Kindled afresh within my memory
The many dear achievements that befell

In those prime years and infancy of love,
Which to describe were but to die in writing;
Ah, those I sought, but vainly, to remove,
And vainly shall, by which I perish living.

And though strong reason hold before mine eyes
The images and forms of worlds past,
Teaching the cause why all those flames that rise
From forms external can no longer last,

Than that those seeming beauties hold in prime,
Love's ground, his essence, and his empery,
All slaves to age, and vassals unto time,
Of which repentance writes the tragedy,

But this my heart's desire could not conceive,
Whose love outflew the fastest flying time,
A beauty that can easily deceive
Th'arrest of years, and creeping age outclimb,

A spring of beauties which time ripeth not
(Time that but works on frail mortality);
A sweetness which woe's wrongs outwipeth not,
Whom love hath chose for his divinity;

A vestal fire that burns but never wasteth,
That loseth nought by giving light to all,
That endless shines eachwhere, and endless lasteth,
Blossoms of pride that can nor fade nor fall.

These were those marvellous perfections,
The parents of my sorrow and my envy,
Most deathful and most violent infections;
These be the tyrants that in fetters tie

Their wounded vassals, yet nor kill nor cure,
But glory in their lasting misery;
That, as her beauties, would our woes should dure.
These be the effects of powerful empery . . .

Yet have these wonders want, which want compassion;
Yet hath her mind some marks of human race;
Yet will she be a woman for a fashion,
So doth she please her virtues to deface.

And like as that immortal power doth seat
An element of waters, to allay
The fiery sunbeams that on earth do beat
And temper by cold night the heat of day,

So hath perfection, which begat her mind,
Added thereto a change of fantasy,
And left her the affections of her kind,
Yet free from ev'ry ev'l but cruelty.

But leave her praise; speak thou of nought but woe;
Write on the tale that Sorrow bids thee tell;
Strive to forget, and care no more to know 215
Thy cares are known, by knowing those too well.

Describe her now as she appears to thee,
Not as she did appear in days fordone.
In love, those things that were no more may be,
For fancy seldom ends where it begun. 220

And as a stream by strong hand bounded in,
From nature's course where it did sometime run
By some small rent or loose part doth begin
To find escape, till it a way hath won;

Doth then all unawares in sunder tear 225
The forced bounds, and, raging, run at large
In th'ancient channels as they wonted were;
Such is of women's love the careful charge,

Held and maintain'd with multitude of woes;
Of long erections such the sudden fall. 230
One hour diverts, one instant overthrows,
For which our lives, for which our fortune's thrall

So many years those joys have dearly bought;
Of which when our fond hopes do most assure,
All is dissolv'd; our labours come to nought, 235
Nor any mark thereof there doth endure:

No more than when small drops of rain do fall
Upon the parched ground by heat updried;
No cooling moisture is perceiv'd at all
Nor any show or sign of wet doth bide. 240

But as the fields, clothed with leaves and flowers,
The banks of roses smelling precious sweet,
Have but their beauty's date and timely hours,
And then, defac'd by winter's cold and sleet,

So far as neither fruit nor form of flower 245
Stays for a witness what such branches bare,
But as time gave, time did again devour,
And chang'd our rising joy to falling care:

So of affection which our youth presented.
When she, that from the sun reaves power and light, 250
Did but decline her beams as discontented,
Converting sweetest days to saddest night,

All droops, all dies, all trodden under dust
The person, place, and passages forgotten;
The hardest steel eaten with softest rust, 255
The firm and solid tree both rent and rotten.

Those thoughts, so full of pleasure and content,
That in our absence were affection's food,
Are razed out and from the fancy rent,
In highest grace and heart's dear care that stood, 260

Are cast for prey to hatred and to scorn, –
Our dearest treasures and our heart's true joys;
The tokens hung on breast and kindly worn
Are now elsewhere dispos'd or held for toys.

And those which then our jealousy remov'd, 265
And others for our sakes then valu'd dear,
The one forgot, the rest are dear belov'd,
When all of ours doth strange or vile appear.

Those streams seem standing puddles, which before
We saw our beauties in, so were they clear; 270
Belphoebe's course is now observ'd no more;

That fair resemblance weareth out of date.
Our ocean seas are but tempestuous waves,
And all things base, that blessed were of late . . .

And as a field, wherein the stubble stands 275
Of harvest past, the ploughman's eye offends;
He tills again, or tears them up with hands,
And throws to fire as foil'd and fruitless ends,

And takes delight another seed to sow;
So doth the mind root up all wonted thought, 280
And scorns the care of our remaining woes;
The sorrows, which themselves for us have wrought,

Are burnt to cinders by new kindled fires;
The ashes are dispers'd into the air;
The sighs, the groans of all our past desires285
Are clean outworn, as things that never were.

With youth is dead the hope of Love's return,
Who looks not back to hear our after-cries:
Where he is not, he laughs at those that mourn;
Whence he is gone, he scorns the mind that dies.290

When he is absent, he believes no words;
When reason speaks, he, careless, stops his ears;
Whom he hath left, he never grace affords,
But bathes his wings in our lamenting tears.

Unlasting passion, soon outworn conceit,295
Whereon I built, and on so dureless trust!
My mind had wounds, I dare not say deceit,
Were I resolv'd her promise was not just.

Sorrow was my revenge and woe my hate;
I powerless was to alter my desire;300
My love is not of time or bound to date.
My heart's internal heat and living fire

Would not, or could, be quench'd with sudden showers;
My bound respect was not confin'd to days;
My vowed faith not set to ended hours.305
I love the bearing and not-bearing sprays

Which now to others do their sweetness send,
Th'incarnate, snow-driv'n white, and pur'st azure,
Who from high heaven doth on their fields descend,
Filling their barns with grain, and towers with treasure.310

Erring or never erring, such is love
As, while it lasteth, scorns th'account of those
Seeking but self-contentment to improve,
And hides, if any be, his inward woes,

And will not know, while he knows his own passion,315
The often and unjust perseverance
In deeds of love and state, and ev'ry action
From that first day and year of their joy's entrance.

But I, unbless'd and ill-born creature,
That did embrace the dust her body bearing, 320
That lov'd her, both by fancy and by nature,
That drew, e'en with the milk in my first sucking,

Affection from the parent's breast that bare me,
Have found her as a stranger so severe,
Improving my mishap in each degree; 325
But love was gone. So would I my life were!

A queen she was to me, no more Belphoebe;
A lion then, no more a milk-white dove;
A prisoner in her breast I could not be; –
She did untie the gentle chains of love. 330

Love was no more the love of hiding
All trespass and mischance for her own glory.
It had been such; it was still for the elect;
But I must be the example in love's story.
This was of all forepast the sad effect. 335

But thou, my weary soul and heavy thought,
Made by her love a burden to my being,
Dost know my error never was forethought,
Or ever could proceed from sense of loving.

Of other cause if then it had proceeding, 340
I leave th'excuse, sith judgment hath been given;
The limbs divided, sunder'd and ableeding,
Cannot complain the sentence was uneven.

This did that Nature's wonder, Virtue's choice,
The only paragon of Time's begetting, 345
Divine in words, angelical in voice,
That spring of joys, that flower of Love's own setting,

Th'idea remaining of those golden ages,
That beauty, braving heavens and earth embalming,
Which after worthless worlds but play on stages, 350
Such didst thou her long since describe, yet sighing

That thy unable spirit could not find aught,
In heaven's beauties or in earth's delight,
For likeness fit to satisfy thy thought:
But what hath it avail'd thee so to write? 355

She cares not for thy praise, who knows not theirs;
It's now an idle labour, and a tale
Told out of time, that dulls the hearer's ears,
A merchandise whereof there is no sale.

Leave them, or lay them up with thy despairs.  360
She hath resolv'd, and judg'd thee long ago.
Thy lines are now a murmuring to her ears,
Like to a falling stream, which, passing slow,

Is wont to nourish sleep and quietness;
So shall thy painful labours be perus'd,  365
And draw on rest, which sometime had regard;
But those her cares thy errors have excus'd.

Thy days fordone have had their day's reward;
So her hard heart, so her estranged mind,
In which above the heavens I once repos'd,  370
So to thy error have her ears inclin'd,

And have forgotten all thy past deserving,
Holding in mind but only thine offence;
And only now affecteth thy depraving,
And thinks all vain that pleadeth thy defence.  375

Yet greater fancy beauty never bred;
A more desire the heart-blood never nourished;
Her sweetness an affection ever fed,
Which more in any age hath never flourished.

The mind and virtue never have begotten  380
A firmer love, since love on earth had power;
A love obscur'd, but cannot be forgotten;
Too great and strong for Time's jaws to devour,

Containing such a faith as ages wound not.
Care, wakeful ever of her good estate,  385
Fear, dreading loss, which sighs, and joys not
A memory of the joys her grace begat,

A lasting gratefulness for those comforts past
Of which the cordial sweetness cannot die –
These thoughts, knit up by faith, shall ever last;  390
These time assays, but never can untie,

Whose life once liv'd in her pearl-like breast,
Whose joys were drawn but from her happiness,
Whose heart's high pleasure and whose mind's true rest
Proceeded from her fortune's blessedness;

Who was intentive, wakeful, and dismay'd
In fears, in dreams, in fev'rous jealousy,
Who long in silence served, and obey'd
With secret heart and hidden loyalty.

Which never change to sad adversity,
Which never age, or nature's overthrow,
Which never sickness or deformity,
Which never wasting care or wearing woe

(If subject unto these she could have been),
Which never words or wits malicious,
Which never honour's bait, or world's fame,
Achieved by attempts adventurous,
Or aught beneath the sun or heaven's frame

Can so dissolve, dissever, or destroy
Th'essential love of no frail parts compounded,
Though of the same now buried be the joy,
The hope, the comfort, and the sweetness ended,

But that the thoughts and memories of these
Work a relapse of passion, and remain
Of my sad heart the sorrow-sucking bees;
The wrongs receiv'd, the frowns persuade in vain.

And though these med'cines work desire to end,
And are in others the true cure of liking,
The salves that heal love's wounds, and do amend
Consuming woe, and slake our hearty sighing,

They work not so in thy mind's long decease.
External fancy time alone recureth,
All whose effects do wear away with ease.
Love of delight, while such delight endureth
Stays by the pleasure, but no longer stays.

But in my mind so is her love inclos'd,
And is thereof not only the best part,
But into it the essence is dispos'd.
O love! (the more my woe) to it thou art

Ev'n as the moisture in each plant that grows, 430
Ev'n as the sun unto the frozen ground,
Ev'n as the sweetness to th'incarnate rose;
Ev'n as the centre in each perfect round:

As water to the fish, to men as air,
As heat to fire, as light unto the sun. 435
Oh love! it is but vain to say *thou were*;
Ages and times cannot thy power outrun.

Thou art the soul of that unhappy mind
Which, being by nature made an idle thought,
Began ev'n then to take immortal kind, 440
When first her virtues in thy spirits wrought.

From thee therefore that mover cannot move,
Because it is become thy cause of being;
Whatever error may obscure that love,
Whatever frail effect of mortal living, 445

Whatever passion from distemper'd heart,
What absence, time, or injuries effect,
What faithless friends or deep dissembled art
Present to feed her most unkind suspect.

Yet as the air in deep caves underground 450
Is strongly drawn when violent heat hath rent
Great clefts therein, till moisture do abound,
And then the same, imprison'd and up-pent,

Breaks out in earthquakes tearing all asunder;
So, in the centre of my cloven heart, 455
My heart, to whom her beauties were such wonder,
Lies the sharp poison'd head of that love's dart,

Which, till all break and all dissolve to dust,
Thence drawn it cannot be, or therein known.
There, mix'd with my heart-blood, the fretting rust 460
The better part hath eaten and outgrown.

But what of those or these? or what of ought
Of that which was, or that which is, to treat?
What I possess is but the same I sought:
My love was false, my labours were deceit.

Nor less than such they are esteem'd to be,
A fraud bought at the price of many woes,
A guile, whereof the profits unto me –
Could it be thought premeditate for those?

Witness those wither'd leaves left on the tree,
The sorrow-worn face, the pensive mind;
Th'external shews what may th'internal be.
Cold care hath bitten both the root and rind.

But stay, my thoughts, make end: give fortune way.
Harsh is the voice of woe and sorrow's sound.
Complaints cure not, and tears do but allay
Griefs for a time, which after more abound.

To seek for moisture in th'Arabian sand
Is but a loss of labour and of rest.
The links which time did break of hearty bands

Words cannot knit, or wailings make anew.
Seek not the sun in clouds when it is set.
On highest mountains, where those cedars grew,
Against whose banks the troubled ocean bett,

And were the marks to find thy hoped port,
Into a soil far off themselves remove.
On Sestus' shore, Leander's late resort,
Hero hath left no lamp to guide her love;

Thou look'st for light in vain, and storms arise;
She sleeps thy death, that erst thy danger sighed.
Strive then no more, bow down thy weary eyes,
Eyes which to all these woes thy heart have guided.

She is gone, she is lost! she is found, she is ever fair!
Sorrow draws weakly, where love draws not too:
Woe's cries sound nothing, but only in love's ear.
Do then by dying what life cannot do.

Unfold thy flocks and leave them to the fields
To feed on hills, or dales, where likes them best,
Of what the summer or the spring-time yields,
For love and time hath given thee leave to rest. 500

Thy heart which was their fold, now in decay
By often storms and winter's many blasts,
All torn and rent becomes misfortune's prey;
False hope my shepherd's staff, now age hath brast.

My pipe, which love's own hand gave my desire 505
To sing her praises and my woe upon,
Despair hath often threaten'd to the fire,
As vain to keep now all the rest are gone.


Thus home I draw, as death's long night draws on;
Yet ev'ry foot, old thoughts turn back mine eyes: 510
Constraint me guides, as old age draws a stone
Against the hill, which over-weighty lies

For feeble arms or wasted strength to move.
My steps are backward, gazing on my loss,
My mind's affection and my soul's sole love, 515
Not mix'd with fancy's chaff or fortune's dross.

To God I leave it, who first gave it me,
And I her gave, and she return'd again,
As it was hers. So let His mercies be
Of my last comforts the essential mean. 520
    But be it so or not, th'effects are past.
    Her love hath end; my woe must ever last.

## 14. The End of the Books of the Ocean's Love to Cynthia, and the Beginning of the Two-and-twentieth Book, entreating of Sorrow

My days' delights, my spring-time joys fordone,
Which in the dawn and rising sun of youth
Had their creation, and were first begun,

Do in the evening and the winter sad
Present my mind, which takes my time's account, 5
The grief remaining of the joy it had.

My times that then ran o'er themselves in these,
And now run out in other's happiness,
Bring unto those new joys and new-born days.

So could she not if she were not the sun, 10
Which sees the birth, and burial, of all else,
And holds that power with which she first begun,

Leaving each wither'd body to be torn
By fortune, and by times tempestuous,
Which, by her virtue, once fair fruit have borne, 15

Knowing she can renew, and can create
Green from the ground, and flowers even out of stone,
By virtue lasting over time and date,

Leaving us only woe, which, like the moss,
Having compassion of unburied bones, 20
Cleaves to mischance, and unrepaired loss.

For tender stalks . . .

## 15. The Lie

Go soul, the body's guest,
Upon a thankless arrant,
Fear not to touch the best,
The truth shall be thy warrant.
    Go, since I needs must die,
    And give the world the lie.

Say to the Court, it glows
And shines like rotten wood,
Say to the Church, it shows
What's good, but doth no good:
    If Church and Court reply,
    Give Court and Church the lie.

Tell potentates, they live
Acting by others' actions,
Not lov'd unless they give,
Not strong but by affections:
    If potentates reply,
    Give potentates the lie.

Tell men of high condition,
That in affairs of state
Their purpose is ambition,
Their practice only hate,
    And if they once reply,
    Then give them all the lie.

Tell them that brave it most,
They beg for more by spending,
Who, in their greatest cost,
Seek nothing but commending:
    And if they make reply,
    Give each of them the lie.

## 15. THE LIE

Tell zeal it wants devotion,
Tell love it is but lust.
Tell time it metes but motion,
Tell flesh it is but dust.
    And wish them not reply,
    For thou must give the lie.

Tell age it daily wasteth,
Tell honour how it alters.
Tell beauty that she blasteth,
Tell favour how it falters.
    And as they shall reply
    Give every one the lie.

Tell wit how much it wrangles
In tickle points of niceness,
Tell wisdom she entangles
Herself in over-wiseness.
    And when they do reply
    Straight give them both the lie.

Tell physic of her boldness,
Tell skill it is prevention,
Tell charity of coldness,
Tell law it is contention,
    And as they do reply
    So give them still the lie.

Tell Fortune of her blindness,
Tell nature of decay,
Tell friendship of unkindness.
Tell justice of delay.
    And if they will reply,
    Then give them all the lie.

Tell arts they have no soundness,
But vary by esteeming;
Tell schools they want profoundness,
And stand too much on seeming.
    If arts and schools reply,
    Give arts and schools the lie.

Tell faith it's fled the city,
Tell how the country erreth,
Tell manhood shakes off pity
And virtue least preferreth.
    And if they do reply,
    Spare not to give the lie.

So when thou hast, as I
Commanded thee, done blabbing,
Although to give the lie
Deserves no less than stabbing,
    Stab at thee he that will,
    No stab the soul can kill.

## 15a. 'Go, echo of the mind, a careless truth protest'

[an answer, possibly by Robert Devereux, Earl of Essex]

Go, echo of the mind, a careless truth protest,
Make answer that so raw a lie no stomach can digest.
For why? The lie's descent is over-base to tell;
To us it came from Italy, to them it came from Hell.
What reason proves, confess; what slander saith, deny; 5
Let no untruth with triumph pass – but never give the lie.
Confess in glittering court all are not gold that shine,
Yet say one pearl and much fine gold grows in that princely mine.
Confess that many tares do overgrow the ground,
Yet say within the field of God good corn is to be found. 10
Confess some judge unjust the widow's right delay,
Yet say there are some Samuels that never say her nay.
Admit some man of state do pitch his thoughts too high;
Is that a rule for all the rest their loyal hearts to try?
Your wits are in the wane, your autumn in the bud, 15
You argue from particulars, your reason is not good.
And still that men may see less reason to commend you,
I marvel most amongst the rest how schools and arts offend you.
But why pursue I thus the weightless words of the wind?
The more the crab doth seek to creep, the more she is behind. 20
In church and commonwealth, in court and country both,
What, nothing good, but all so bad that ev'ry man doth loathe?
The further that you range your error is the wider;
The bee sometimes doth honey suck, but sure you are a spider.
And so my counsel is, for that you want a name, 25
To seek some corner in the dark to hide yourself from shame.
There wrap the silly fly within your spiteful web –
Both church and court may want you well, they are at no such ebb.
As quarrels once begun are not so quickly ended,
So many faults may soon be found but not so soon amended. 30
And when you come again to give the world the lie,
I pray you tell them how to live and teach them how to die.

## 16. 'Nature, that wash'd her hands in milk'

Nature, that wash'd her hands in milk
    And had forgot to dry them,
Instead of earth took snow and silk
    At Love's request, to try them
If she a mistress could compose
To please Love's fancy out of those.

Her eyes he would should be of light,
    A violet breath and lips of jelly,
Her hair not black nor over-bright,
    And of the softest down her belly;
As for her inside he'd have it
Only of wantonness and wit.

At Love's entreaty, such a one
    Hath Nature made, but with her beauty
She hath fram'd a heart of stone,
    So as Love by his ill destiny
Must die for her whom Nature gave him
Because her darling would not save him.

But Time, which Nature doth despise
    And rudely gives her love the lie,
Makes Hope a fool, Sorrow wise,
    His hands doth neither wash nor dry
But, being made of steel and rust,
Turns snow and silk and milk to dust.

The light, the belly, lips and breath,
    He dims, discolours and destroys;
With those he feeds but fills not Death,
    Which sometime were the food of joys.
Yea, Time doth dull each lively wit
And dries all wantonness with it.

O cruel Time, which takes in trust
    Our youth, our joys and all we have,
And pays us but with age and dust,
    Who in the dark and silent grave
When we have wander'd all our ways
Shuts up the story of our days.

## 17. 'What is our life? It is a play of passion'

What is our life? It is a play of passion.
What is our mirth? The music of division.
Our mothers, they the tiring-houses be,
Where we are dress'd for time's short tragedy.
Earth is the stage, heaven the spectator is
Who doth behold whoe'er doth act amiss.
The graves that hide us from the parching sun
Are but drawn curtains till the play is done.

## 18. To the Translator of Lucan

Had Lucan hid the truth to please the time
He had been too unworthy of thy pen,
Who never sought nor ever car'd to climb
By flattery, or seeking worthless men.
For this thou hast been bruis'd; but yet those scars
Do beautify no less than those wounds do
Receiv'd in just and in religious wars;
Though thou hast bled by both, and bear'st them too.
Change not! To change thy fortune 'tis too late.
Who with a manly faith resolves to die,
May promise to himself a lasting state,
Though not so great, yet free from infamy.
    Such was thy Lucan, whom so to translate,
    Nature thy muse like Lucan's did create.

## 19. A Petition to Queen Anne

My day's delight, my spring-time joys fordone,
Which in the dawn and rising sun of youth
Had their creation and were first begun,

Do in the evening and the winter sad
Present my mind, which takes my time's account,
The griefs remaining of the joy it had.

My tender stalks, now clad with rugged rinds,
Whose former fruit was of such mixture made
As with the harmful blast and eastern wind

In crept the eating worm, and in the heart
And kernel taketh nourishment
Till it had all devour'd the better part;

Which when my wants presented to my taste,
Then hopeful of the good mine own hands planted
Of all my toil I found false fruit at last,

Love all eaten out but in outward show,
My elder fortune cut by new mishap,
The false internal then I only knew.

For as no fortune stands, so no man's love
Stays by the wretched and disconsolate;
All old affections from new sorrows move.

Moss by unburied bones, ivy by walls,
Whom life and people have abandon'd,
Till th'one be rotten stays, till th'other falls;

But friendships, kindred and love's memory
Die, cool, extinguish, hearing or beholding
The voice of woe or face of misery.

For friends in all are like those winter showers
Which come uncall'd, but then forebear to fall
When harmful heat hath burnt both leaves and flowers.

Then what we sometime were they know no more
Whenas those storms of powerful destiny
Have once defac'd the form we had before.

For if there did in cinders but remain
The smallest heat of love's long-lasting fires  35
I could not call for right and call in vain,

Or, had truth power, the guiltless could not fall,
Malice win glory or revenge triumph.
But truth alone cannot encounter all.

All love, and all desert of former times  40
Malice hath cover'd from my sov'reign's eyes
And largely abroad suspected crimes,

Burying the former with their memory,
Teaching Offence to speak before it go,
Disguising private hate with public duty.  45

Cold walls, to you I sigh, but you are senseless,
Yet senseful all alike as are those friends,
Friends only of my sometime happiness.

To whom then shall I cry? to whom shall wrong
Cast down her tears or hold up folded hands?  50
To her to whom compassion doth belong,

To her who is the first, and may alone
Be called Empress of the Brittannies.
Who should have mercy if a queen have none?

Who can resist strong hate, fierce injury?  55
Or who relieve th'oppressed state of truth
Who is companion else to powerful majesty?

But you, great, goodliest, graceful princess,
Who hath brought glory and prosperity
Unto a widow's land and people hopeless,  60

Perfect our comfort by protecting those
Whom hate and no self-guile hath ruin'd.
All in the field are yours, whatever grows,

As well the humble briar under shade
As are the tallest cedars which obscure them.  65
Love, Nature, Right have you their princess made;

Save then your own, whose life in your defence
I scorn'd to keep and could have joy'd to lose;
For love, destruction is no recompense.

If I have sold my duty, sold my faith
To strangers, which was only due to one,
Nothing I should esteem as dear as death,

But if both God and time shall make you know
That I, your humble vassal, am oppress'd,
Then cast your eyes on undeserved woe,

That I and mine may never mourn the miss
Of her we had, but praise our living Queen
Who brings us equal, if no greater, bliss.

## 20. 'My broken pipes shall on the willow hang'

My broken pipes shall on the willow hang,
Like those which on the Babylonian banks,
Their joys foredone, their present sorrow sang
– These times to worth yielding but frozen thanks.

## 21. 'Ev'n such is time, which takes in trust'

Ev'n such is time, which takes in trust
Our youth, our joys and all we have,
And pays us but with age and dust;
Who in the dark and silent grave
When we have wander'd all our ways 5
Shuts up the story of our days.
  And from which earth and grave and dust
  The Lord shall raise me up, I trust.

## 22. Verse Translations from *The History of the World*

i. 'Albinovanus', *Eleg. de ob. Maec.*, 113–4

The plants and trees, made poor and old
By winter envious,
The spring-time bounteous
Covers again from shame and cold;
But never man repair'd again						5
His youth and beauty lost,
Though art and care and cost
Do promise nature's help in vain.

ii. Ausonius, *Epigrams*, cxviii

I am that Dido which thou here dost see
Cunningly fram'd in beauteous imagery.
Like this I was, but had not such a soul
As Maro feign'd, incestuous and foul.
Aeneas never with his Trojan host						5
Beheld my face, or landed on this coast;
But flying proud Iarbas' villainy,
Not mov'd by furious love or jealousy,
I did, with weapon chaste, to save my fame,
Make way for death untimely ere it came.						10
This was my end. But first I built a town,
Reveng'd my husband's death, liv'd with renown.
Why didst thou stir up Vergil, envious Muse,
Falsely my name and honour to abuse?
Readers, believe historians; not those						15
Which to the world Jove's thefts and vice expose.
Poets are liars; and for verses' sake,
Will make the gods of human crimes partake.

iii. Catullus, v.4–6

The sun may set and rise,
But we, contrariwise,

Sleep, after our short light,
One everlasting night.

iv. Horace, *Odes*, III.xvi.1–11

The brazen tower, with doors close barr'd
And watchful bandogs' frightful guard,
      Kept safe the maidenhead
Of Danae from secret love,
Till smiling Venus and wise Jove                     5
      Beguil'd her father's dread:
For, chang'd into a golden shower,
The god into her lap did pour
      Himself and took his pleasure.
Through guards and stony walls to break              10
The thunderbolt is far more weak
      Than is a golden treasure.

v. Horace, *Odes*, IV.ix.25–8

Many by valour have deserv'd renown
      Ere Agamemnon, yet lie all oppress'd
Under long night, unwept for and unknown;
      For with no sacred poet were they blest.

vi. Juvenal, xv.9–11

Th'Egyptians think it sin to root up or to bite
Their leeks or onions, which they serve with holy rite.
O happy nations, which of their own sowing
Have store of gods in every garden growing!

vii. Lucan, *Pharsalia*, iv.131–5

The moisten'd osier of the hoary willow
Is woven first into a little boat;
Then, cloth'd in bullock's hide, upon the billow
Of a proud river lightly doth it float
      Under the waterman:                            5
So on the lakes of overswelling Po
Sails the Venetian; and the Briton so
      On th'outspread ocean.

viii. 'Orpheus'

Then, marking this my sacred speech, but truly lend
Thy heart that's reason's sphere, and the right way ascend,
And see the world's sole king. First, he is simply one
Begotten of himself, from whom is born alone
All else, in which he's still; nor could it e'er befall          5
A mortal eye to see him once, yet he sees all.

ix. 'Orpheus'

The first of all is God, and the same last is he.
God is the head and midst; yea, from him all things be.
God is the base of earth and of the starred sky;
He is the male and female too; shall never die.
The spirit of all is God; the sun and moon and what
    is higher;                                                  5
The king, the original of all, of all the end:
For close in holy breast he all did comprehend;
Whence all to blessed light His wondrous power did send.

x. Pausanias vii.xii.1

One fire than other burns more forcibly,
One wolf than other wolves does bite more sore,
One hawk more swift than other hawks does fly.
So one most mischievous of men before,
Callicrates, false knave as knave might be,                      5
Met with Menalcidas, more false than he.

xi. Vergil, *Aeneid*, iii.104–12

In the main sea the isle of Crete doth lie
Whence Jove was born; thence is our progeny.
There is Mount Ida; there in fruitful land
An hundred great and goodly cities stand.
Thence, if I follow not mistaken fame,                           5
Teucer, the eldest of our grandsires, came
To the Rhoetean shores, and reigned there
Ere yet fair Ilion was built, and ere
The towers of Troy. Their dwelling-place they sought
In lowest vales. Hence Cybel's rites were brought;              10

Hence Corybantian cymbals did remove;
And hence the name of our Idaean grove.

xii. Vergil, *Aeneid*, vi.724–7

The heaven and earth and all the liquid main,
The moon's bright globe and stars Titanian,
A spirit within maintains; and their whole mass
A mind, which through each part infus'd doth pass,
Fashions and works, and wholly doth transpierce
All this great body of the universe.

# II

# Poems Sometimes Attributed to Sir Walter Ralegh

## 23. 'Sweet are the thoughts where Hope persuadeth Hap'

Sweet are the thoughts where Hope persuadeth Hap,
Great are the joys where Heart obtains request,
Dainty the life nurs'd still in Fortune's lap,
Much is the ease where troubled minds find rest.
These are the fruits that valour doth advance 5
And cuts off dread by hope of happy chance.

Thus hope brings hap but to the worthy wight,
Thus pleasure comes but after hard assay,
Thus fortune yields in mauger of her spite,
Thus happy state is won without delay. 10
Then must I needs advance myself by skill,
And live to serve in hope of your good will.

## 24. A Poem put into my Lady Leighton's Pocket

Lady, farewell, whom I in silence serve;
    Would God thou knew'st the depth of my desire.
Then might I hope, though nought I can deserve,
    Some drop of grace would quench my scorching fire.
But as to love unknown I have decreed,
So spare to speak doth often spare to speed.

Yet better 'twere that I in woe should waste
    Than sue for grace and pity in despite,
And though I see in thee such pleasure plac'd
    That feeds my joy and breeds my chief delight,
Withall I see a chaste content disdain
Their suits which seek to win thy will again.

Then farewell hope and help to each man's harm,
    The wind of woe hath torn my tree of trust.
Care quench'd the coals which did my fancy warm
    And all my help lies buried in the dust.
But yet amongst those cares which cross my rest
This comfort grows; I think I love thee best.

## 25. A Poesy to Prove Affection is not Love

Conceit begotten by the eyes
Is quickly born and quickly dies;
For while it seeks our hearts to have,
Meanwhile, there reason makes his grave;
For many things the eyes approve,
Which yet the heart doth seldom love.

For as the seeds in spring time sown
Die in the ground ere they be grown,
Such is conceit, whose rooting fails,
As child that in the cradle quails
Or else within the mother's womb
Hath his beginning and his tomb.

Affection follows Fortune's wheels,
And soon is shaken from her heels,
For, following beauty or estate,
Her liking still is turn'd to hate.
For all affections have their change,
And fancy only loves to range.

Desire himself runs out of breath,
And, getting, doth but gain his death:
Desire nor reason hath nor rest,
And, blind, doth seldom choose the best.
Desire attain'd is not desire,
But as the cinders of the fire.

As ships in ports desir'd are drown'd,
As fruit, once ripe, then falls to ground,
As flies that seek for flames are brought
To cinders by the flames they sought;
So fond desire when it attains,
The life expires, the woe remains.

And yet some poets fain would prove
Affection to be perfect love,
And that desire is of that kind,
No less a passion of the mind,
As if wild beasts and men did seek
To like, to love, to choose alike.

## 26. 'Passions are liken'd best to floods and streams'

Passions are liken'd best to floods and streams;
The shallow murmur, but the deep are dumb.
So when affection yields discourse, it seems
The bottom is but shallow whence they come.
      They that are rich in words, in words discover 5
      That they are poor in that which makes a lover.

## 27. Sir Walter Ralegh to his Son

Three things there be that prosper all apace
And flourish while they are asunder far,
But on a day, they meet all in a place,
And when they meet, they one another mar.

And they be these; the Wood, the Weed, the Wag:
The Wood is that that makes the gallows tree;
The Weed is that that strings the hangman's bag;
The Wag, my pretty knave, betokens thee.

Now mark, dear boy, while these assemble not,
Green springs the tree, hemp grows, the wag is wild;
But when they meet, it makes the timber rot,
It frets the halter, and it chokes the child.

## 28. The Passionate Man's Pilgrimage

Give me my scallop shell of quiet,
My staff of faith to walk upon,
My scrip of joy, immortal diet,
My bottle of salvation,
My gown of glory, hope's true gage,  5
And thus I'll take my pilgrimage.

Blood must be my body's balmer,
No other balm will there be given,
Whilst my soul, like quiet palmer,
Travelleth towards the land of heaven  10
Over the silver mountains,
Where spring the nectar fountains.
There will I kiss
The bowl of bliss,
And drink my eternal fill  15
On every milken hill.
My soul will be adry before,
But after, it will thirst no more.

Then by the happy blissful way
More peaceful pilgrims I shall see,  20
That have cast off their rags of clay,
And go apparell'd fresh like me.
I'll bring them first
To quench their thirst
And then to taste of nectar suckets,  25
At the clear wells
Where sweetness dwells,
Drawn up by saints in crystal buckets.

And when our bottles and all we
Are fill'd with immortality,  30
Then the holy paths we'll travel,
Strew'd with rubies thick as gravel;
Ceilings of diamonds, sapphire floors,
High walls of coral, pearl bowers.

From thence to heaven's bribeless hall, 35
Where no corrupted voices brawl,
No conscience molten into gold,
No forg'd accuser bought and sold,
No cause deferr'd, no vain-spent journey,
For there Christ is the King's Attorney, 40
Who pleads for all without degrees,
And he hath angels, but no fees.
And when the grand twelve-million jury
Of our sins with direful fury
Against our souls black verdicts give, 45
Christ pleads His death, and then we live.
Be Thou my speaker, taintless pleader,
Unblotted lawyer, true proceeder;
Thou mov'st salvation ev'n for alms,
Not with a bribed lawyer's palms. 50

And this is mine eternal plea
To him that made heaven, earth, and sea,
Seeing my flesh must die so soon,
And want a head to dine next noon,
Just at the stroke, when my veins start and spread, 55
Set on my soul an everlasting head.
Then am I ready, like a palmer fit,
To tread those blest paths which before I writ.

## 29. 'As you came from the holy land'

As you came from the holy land
    Of Walsingham,
Met you not with my true love
    By the way as you came?

How shall I know your true love,
    That have met many one,
As I went to the holy land,
    That have come, that have gone?

She is neither white nor brown,
    But as the heavens fair;
There is none hath a form so divine
    In the earth or the air.

Such an one did I meet, good sir,
    Such an angelic face,
Who like a queen, like a nymph, did appear,
    By her gait, by her grace.

She hath left me here all alone,
    All alone, as unknown,
Who sometimes did me lead with herself,
    And me lov'd as her own.

What's the cause that she leaves you alone
    And a new way doth take,
Who lov'd you once as her own,
    And her joy did you make?

I have lov'd her all my youth,
    But now old, as you see.
Love likes not the falling fruit
    From the wither'd tree.

Know that Love is a careless child,
    And forgets promise past;
He is blind, he is deaf when he list,
    And in faith never fast.

His desire is a dureless content,
    And a trustless joy;
He is won with a world of despair,
    And is lost with a toy.

Of womenkind such indeed is the love,
    Or the word 'love' abus'd,
Under which many childish desires
    And conceits are excus'd.

But true love is a durable fire,
    In the mind ever burning,
Never sick, never old, never dead,
    From itself never turning.

## 30a. The Passionate Shepherd to his Love [by Christopher Marlowe]

Come live with me and be my love
And we will all the pleasures prove
That vallies, groves, hills and fields,
Woods or steepy mountains yields.

And we will sit upon the rocks,
Seeing the shepherds feed their flocks
By shallow rivers to whose falls
Melodious birds sing madrigals.

And I will make thee beds of roses
And a thousand fragrant posies
A cap of flowers, and a kirtle
Embroider'd all with leaves of myrtle;

A gown made of the finest wool
Which from our pretty lambs we pull;
Fair lined slippers for the cold,
With buckles of the purest gold;

A belt of straw and ivy buds
With coral clasps and amber studs;
And if these pleasures may thee move,
Come live with me and be my love.

## 30. The Nymph's reply to the Shepherd

If all the world and love were young
And truth in ev'ry shepherd's tongue,
These pretty pleasures might me move
To live with thee and be thy love.

Time drives the flocks from field to fold,
When rivers rage and rocks grow cold,
And Philomel becometh dumb;
The rest complains of cares to come.

The flowers do fade, and wanton fields
To wayward winter reckoning yields:
A honey tongue, a heart of gall,
Is fancy's spring, but sorrow's fall.

Thy gowns, thy shoes, thy beds of roses,
Thy cap, thy kirtle, and thy posies,
Soon break, soon wither, soon forgotten,
In folly ripe, in reason rotten.

Thy belt of straw and ivy buds,
Thy coral clasps and amber studs,
All these in me no means can move
To come to thee and be thy love.

But could youth last, and love still breed,
Had joys no date, nor age no need,
Then those delights my mind might move
To live with thee and be thy love.

## 31. The Advice

Many desire, but few or none deserve
To win the fort of thy most constant will;
Therefore take heed; let fancy never swerve
But unto him that will defend thee still.
    For this be sure, the fort of fame once won,
    Farewell the rest, thy happy days are done.

Many desire, but few or none deserve
To pluck the flowers and let the leaves to fall;
Therefore take heed; let fancy never swerve
But unto him that will take leaves and all.
    For this be sure, the flower once pluck'd away,
    Farewell the rest, thy happy days decay.

Many desire, but few or none deserve
To cut the corn not subject to the sickle;
Therefore take heed; let fancy never swerve,
But constant stand, for mowers' minds are fickle;
    For this be sure, the crop being once obtain'd,
    Farewell the rest, the soil will be disdain'd.

## 32. 'Prais'd be Diana's fair and harmless light'

Prais'd be Diana's fair and harmless light,
Prais'd be the dews wherewith she moists the ground;
Prais'd be her beams, the glory of the night,
Prais'd be her power, by which all powers abound.

Prais'd be her nymphs, with whom she decks the woods, 5
Prais'd be her knights, in whom true honour lives,
Prais'd be that force by which she moves the floods;
Let that Diana shine which all these gives.

In heaven queen she is among the spheres;
She mistress-like makes all things to be pure. 10
Eternity in her oft change she bears.
She beauty is; by her the fair endure.

Time wears her not; she doth his chariot guide.
Mortality below her orb is plac'd,
By her the virtues of the stars down slide, 15
In her is virtue's perfect image cast.

    A knowledge pure it is her worth to know:
    With Circes let them dwell that think not so.

## 33. 'Like to a hermit poor in place obscure'

Like to a hermit poor in place obscure
I mean to spend my days of endless doubt,
To wail such woes as time cannot recure,
Where nought but Love shall ever find me out.

My food shall be of care and sorrow made;  5
My drink nought else but tears fall'n from mine eyes;
And for my light, in such obscured shade,
The flames shall serve which from my heart arise.

A gown of grief my body shall attire,
My staff of broken hope whereon I'll stay;  10
Of late repentance link'd with long desire
The couch is fram'd whereon my limbs I'll lay.
    And at my gates Despair shall linger still,
      To let in Death when Love and Fortune will.

## 34. 'Feed still thyself, thou fondling, with belief'

Feed still thyself, thou fondling, with belief,
Go hunt thy hope that never took effect,
Accuse the wrongs that oft hath wrought thy grief
And reckon sure where reason would suspect.

Dwell in the dreams of wish and vain desire,
Pursue the faith that flies and seeks to new,
Run after hopes that mock thee with retire
And look for love where liking never grew.

Devise conceits to ease thy careful heart,
Trust upon times and days of grace behind,
Presume the rights of promise and desert
And measure love by thy believing mind.

Force thy affects that spite doth daily chase,
Wink at thy wrongs with wilful oversight,
See not the soil and stain of thy disgrace,
Nor reck disdain, to dote on thy delight.

And when thou seest the end of thy reward,
And these effects ensue of thine assault,
When rashness rues that reason should regard,
Yet still accuse thy fortune for the fault

    And cry, O love, O death, O vain desire,
    When thou complain'st the heat and feeds the fire.

## 35. 'My first-born love, unhappily conceiv'd'

My first-born love, unhappily conceiv'd,
Brought forth in pain and christen'd with a curse,
Die in your infancy, of life bereav'd
        By your cruel nurse.

Restless desire that from my love proceeded, 5
Leave to be, and seek your heaven by dying,
Since you, O you, your own hope have exceeded
        By too high flying.

And you, my words, my heart's faithful expounders,
No more offer your jewel unesteem'd, 10
Since those eyes, my love's life and lives' confounders,
        Your worth misdeem'd.

Love, leave to desire, words, leave it to utter,
Swell on, my thoughts, till you break that contains you;
My complaints in those deaf ears no more mutter 15
        That so disdains you.

And you, careless of me, without feeling,
With dry eyes behold my tragedy smiling;
Deck your proud triumphs with your poor slave's yielding
        To his own spoiling. 20

But if that wrong or holy truth despised
To just revenge the heavens ever mov'd,
So let her love and be still denied,
        Who she so lov'd.

## 36. 'Those eyes which set my fancy on a fire'

Those eyes which set my fancy on a fire,
Those crisped hairs which hold my heart in chains,
Those dainty hands which conquer'd my desire,
That wit, which of my thought doth hold the reins;

Those eyes for clearness do the stars surpass,
Those hairs obscure the brightness of the sun,
Those hands more white than ever iv'ry was,
That wit ev'n to the skies hath glory won.

O eyes that pierce our hearts without remorse,
O hairs of right that wears a royal crown,
O hands that conquer more than Caesar's force,
O wit that turns huge kingdoms upside down!

    Then Love be judge, what heart may thee withstand –
    Such eyes, such hair, such wit and such a hand.

## 37. 'A secret murder hath been done of late'

A secret murder hath been done of late,
Unkindness found to be the bloody knife,
And she that did the deed a dame of state,
Fair, gracious, wise as any beareth life.

To quit herself this answer did she make:
'Mistrust,' quoth she, 'hath brought him to this end,
Which makes the man so much himself mistake
To lay the guilt unto his guiltless friend.'

Lady, not so; not fear'd I found my death,
For no desert thus murder'd is my mind;
And yet before I yield my fainting breath
I quit the killer though I blame the kind.

>   You kill, unkind; I die, and yet am true.
>   For at your sight my wound doth bleed anew.

## 38. 'Sought by the world, and hath the world disdain'd'

Sought by the world, and hath the world disdain'd,
Is she, my heart, for whom thou dost endure,
Unto whose grace, sith Kings have not obtain'd,
Sweet is thy choice though loss of life be sour;
    Yet to the man whose youth such pains must prove 5
    No better end than that which comes by love.

Steer then thy course unto the port of death,
Sith thy hard hap no better hap may find,
Where when thou shalt unlade thy latest breath
Envy herself shall swim to save thy mind 10
    Whose body sunk in search to gain that shore
    Where many a prince had perished before.

And yet, my heart, it might have been foreseen,
Since skilful med'cines mends each kind of grief,
Then in my breast full safely hadst thou been; 15
But thou, my heart, wouldst never me believe,
    Who told thee true when first thou didst aspire
    Death was the end of ev'ry such desire.

## 39. 'What else is hell but loss of blissful heaven?'

What else is hell but loss of blissful heaven?
What darkness but lacks of lightsome day?
What else is death but things of life beriv'n?
What winter else but pleasant spring's decay?

Unrest what else but fancy's hot desire, 5
Fed with delay and follow'd with despair?
What else mishap but longing to aspire,
To strive against earth, water, fire and air?

Heaven were my state and happy sunshine day,
And life most blest, to joy one hour's desire; 10
Hap, bliss and rest and sweet springtime of May
Were to behold my fair consuming fire.

> But lo, I feel, by absence from your sight,
> Mishap, unrest, death, winter, hell, dark night.

## 40. On the Cards and the Dice

Before the sixth day of the next new year
Strange wonders in this kingdom shall appear:
Four kings shall be assembled in this isle,
Where they shall keep great tumult for a while.
Many men then shall have an end of crosses,
And many likewise shall sustain great losses;
Many that now full joyful are and glad
Shall at that time be sorrowful and sad.
Full many a Christian's heart shall quake for fear,
The dreadful sound of trump when he shall hear.
Dead bones shall then be tumbled up and down,
In every city and in ev'ry town.
By day or night this tumult shall not cease,
Until an herald shall proclaim a peace,
An herald strange, the like was never born,
Whose very beard is flesh and mouth is horn.

## 41. Sir W. Ralegh on the Snuff of a Candle the Night before he Died

Cowards fear to die, but courage stout,
Rather than live in snuff, will be put out.

# III

# Poems from the Court of Elizabeth I

# ELIZABETH I
# QUEEN OF ENGLAND

## 42. 'A hapless kind of life is this I wear'

A hapless kind of life is this I wear;
Much watch I dure and weary toiling days.
I serve the rout and all their follies bear,
I suffer pride and sup full hard assays.
To others' will my life is all address'd 5
And no way so as might content me best.

## 42a. 'Madam, but mark the labours of our life'

[an answer by Sir Thomas Heneage]

Madam, but mark the labours of our life
And therewithall what errors we be in;
We sue and seek with prayers, stir and strife
Upon this earth a happy state to win,

And whilst with cares we travail to content us 5
In vain desires, and set no certain scope,
We reap but things whereof we oft repent us,
And feed our wills with much-beguiling hope.

We pray for honours lapp'd in Danger's hands,
We strive for riches which we straight forego; 10
We seek delight that all in poison stands,
And set with pains but seeds of sin and woe.

    Then, noble lady, need we not to pray
    The Lord of all for better state and stay?

## 43. 'The doubt of future foes exiles my present joy'

The doubt of future foes exiles my present joy,
And wit warns me to shun such snares as threaten mine annoy,
For falsehood now doth flow, and subjects' faith doth ebb,
Which should not be if Reason rul'd or Wisdom weav'd the web.
But clouds of joy untried do cloak aspiring minds, 5
Which turn to rain of late repent by changed course of winds.
The top of hope suppos'd, the root uprear'd shall be,
And fruitless all their grafted guile, as shortly ye shall see.
The dazzled eyes with pride, which great Ambition blinds,
Shall be unseal'd by worthy wights whose foresight
    falsehood finds. 10
The daughter of Debate that discord aye doth sow
Shall reap no gain where former rule still peace hath
    taught to know.
No foreign banish'd wight shall anchor in this port.
Our realm brooks not seditious sects; let them elsewhere resort.
My rusty sword through rest shall first his edge employ 15
To poll their tops that seek such change or gape for future joy.

## 44. On Monsieur's Departure

I grieve, and dare not show my discontent;
I love, and yet am forc'd to seem to hate.
I do, yet dare not say I ever meant;
I seem stark mute but inwardly do prate.
    I am and not, I freeze and yet am burn'd
    Since from myself another self I turn'd.

My care is like my shadow in the sun,
Follows me flying, flies when I pursue it,
Stands and lies by me, doth what I have done.
His too familiar care doth make me rue it.
    No means I find to rid him from my breast,
    Till by the end of things it be suppress'd.

Some gentler passion slide into my mind,
For I am soft and made of melting snow;
Or be more cruel, Love, and so be kind;
Let me or float or sink, be high or low.
    Or let me live with some more sweet content,
    Or die and so forget what love e'er meant.

## 45. 'Now leave and let me rest'

Now leave and let me rest,
Dame Pleasure, be content;
Go choose among the best,
My doting days be spent.
By sundry signs I see
The proffers are but vain,
And Wisdom warneth me
That Pleasure asketh pain.

And Nature that doth know
How time her steps doth try
Gives place to painful woe
And bids me learn to die,
Since all fair earthly things
Soon ripe will soon be rot,
And all that pleasant springs
Soon wither'd, soon forgot.

And youth that yields new joys
That wanton lust desires
In age repents the toys
That reckless youth requires;
All which delights I leave
To such as folly trains
By pleasure to deceive
Till they do feel the pains.

And from vain pleasures past
I fly and fain would know
The happy life at last
Whereto I hope to go,
For words or wise reports
Or yet examples gone
Can bridle youthful sports
Till age comes stealing on.

The pleasant courtly games
That I delighted in,
Mine elder age now shames 35
Such follies to begin,
And all the fancies strange
That fond delight brought forth
I do intend to change
And count them nothing worth. 40

For I by process worn
Am taught to know the skill,
What might have been forborne
In my young reckless will,
By which good proof I fleet 45
From will to wit again,
In hope to set my feet
In surety to remain.

## ROBERT DEVEREUX
## EARL OF ESSEX

# 46. 'Seated between the old world and the new'

Seated between the old world and the new,
A land there is no other land may touch,
Where reigns a queen in peace and honour true.
Stories or fables do describe no such;
Never did Atlas such a burden bear
As she, in holding up the world oppress'd,
Supplying with her virtue ev'rywhere
Weakness of friends, errors of servants best.

No nation breeds a warmer blood for war,
And yet she calms them with her majesty;
No age hath ever wit refin'd so far,
And yet she calms them by her policy.
    To her thy son must make his sacrifice
    If he will have the morning of his eyes.

## 47. 'Change thy mind since she doth change'

Change thy mind since she doth change,
Let not Fancy still abuse thee;
Thy untruth cannot seem strange
When her falsehood doth excuse thee.
  Love is dead and thou art free;      5
  She doth live but dead to thee.

Whilst she lov'd thee best a while,
See how she hath still delay'd thee,
Using shows for to beguile
Those vain hopes that have betray'd thee.     10
  Now thou sees, although too late,
  Love loves truth, which women hate.

Love no more since she is gone;
She is gone and loves another.
Being once deceiv'd by one,         15
Leave her love but love none other.
  She was false, bid her adieu;
  She was best but yet untrue.

Love, farewell, more dear to me
Than my life which thou preservest;      20
Life, all joys are gone from thee,
Others have what thou deservest.
  O my death doth spring from hence;
  I must die for her offence.

Die, but yet before thou die         25
Make her know what she hath gotten;
She in whom my hopes did lie
Now is chang'd, I quite forgotten.
  She is chang'd but changed base,
  Baser in so vile a place.         30

## 48. 'To plead my faith where faith hath no reward'

To plead my faith where faith hath no reward.
To move remorse where favour is not borne,
To heap complaints which she doth not regard
Were fruitless, bootless, vain, and yields but scorn.
I loved her whom all the world admir'd.   5
I was refus'd of her that can love none,
And my vain hopes which far too high aspir'd
Are dead and buried and forever gone.
Forget my name since you have scorn'd my love
And woman-like do not too late lament.   10
Since for your sake I must all mischief prove,
I none accuse nor nothing do repent.
    I was as fond as ever she was fair,
    Yet lov'd I not more than I now despair.

## 49. 'Happy were he could finish forth his fate'

Happy were he could finish forth his fate
In some unhaunted desert most obscure
From all society, from love, from hate
Of worldly folk! Then should he sleep secure,
Then wake again, and yield God ever praise,  5
Content with hips and haws and brambleberry,
In contemplation passing still his days
And change of holy thoughts to make him merry,
    Who, when he dies, his tomb may be a bush
    Where harmless robin dwells with gentle thrush.  10

## 50. Verses Made by the Earl of Essex in his Trouble

The ways on earth have paths and turnings known,
The ways on sea are gone by needle's light.
The birds of th'air the nearest way have flown
And under earth the moles do cast aright.
A way more hard than these I needs must take
Where none can teach nor no man can direct;
Where no man's good for me example makes,
But all men's faults do teach her to suspect.
Her thoughts and mine such disproportion have;
All strength of love is infinite in me,
She us'th th'advantage time and fortune gave
Of worth and power to get the liberty.
      Earth, sea, heaven, hell are subject unto laws.
      But I, poor I, must suffer and know no cause.

## 51. 'I am not as I seem, I seem and am the same'

I am not as I seem, I seem and am the same.
I am as divers deem, but not as others name.
I am not as I should, I should be as I say;
In wanting what I would, I must be as I may.

## EDWARD DE VERE
## EARL OF OXFORD

# 52. 'I am not as I seem to be'

I am not as I seem to be,
Nor when I smile I am not glad;
A thrall, although you count me free,
I most in mirth most pensive sad.
I smile to shade my bitter spite,
As Hannibal, that saw in sight
His country soil, with Carthage town,
By Roman force defaced down.

And Caesar that presented was
With noble Pompey's princely head
As 'twere some judge to rule the case,
A flood of tears he seem'd to shed.
Although indeed it sprung of joy
Yet others thought it was annoy;
Thus contraries be us'd I find
Of wise to cloak the covert mind.

I Hannibal that smiles for grief,
And let you Caesar's tears suffice:
The one that laughs at his mischief,
The other all for joy that cries.
I smile to see me scorned so,
You weep for joy to see me woe,
And I a heart by love slain dead
Presents in place of Pompey's head.

O cruel hap and hard estate
That forceth me to love my foe,
Accursed by so foul a fate
My choice for to prefix it so,
So long to fight with secret sore
And find no secret salve therefore.
Some purge their pain by plaint, I find,
But I in vain do breathe my wind.

## 53. 'The lively lark stretch'd forth her wing'

The lively lark stretch'd forth her wing,
    The messenger of morning bright,
And with her cheerful voice did sing
    The day's approach discharging night,
When that Aurora blushing red 5
    Descried the guilt of Thetis' bed.

I went abroad to take the air, and in the meads I met a knight,
Clad in carnation colour fair. I did salute this gentle wight,
    Of him I did his name enquire.
    He sighed, and said he was Desire. 10
Desire I did desire to stay; awhile with him I crav'd to talk.

The courteous knight said me no nay, but hand in hand
        with me did walk
    Then of Desire I ask'd again
    What things did please and what did pain.
He smil'd, and thus he answer'd then: 'Desire can have no
        greater pain 15
Than for to see another man that he desireth to obtain,
    Nor greater joy can be than this,
    That to enjoy that others miss.'

## 54. 'When wert thou born, Desire?'

When wert thou born, Desire?
    In pomp and prime of May.
By whom, sweet boy, wert thou begot?
    By Good Conceit, men say.
Tell me who was thy nurse?                            5
    Fresh Youth in sugar'd joy.
What was thy meat and daily food?
    Sad sighs with great annoy.
What hadst thou then to drink?
    Unfeigned lover's tears.                           10
What cradle wert thou rock'd in?
    In hope devoid of fears.
What brought thee then asleep?
    Sweet speech, that lik'd me best.
And where is now thy dwelling-place?            15
    In gentle hearts I rest.
Doth company displease?
    It doth in many a one.
Where would Desire then choose to be?
    He likes to muse alone.                          20
What feedeth most your sight?
    To gaze on Favour still.
What find'st thou most to be thy foe?
    Disdain of my good will.
Will ever age or death                               25
    Bring thee unto decay?
No, no, Desire both lives and dies
    Ten thousand times a day.

## SIR THOMAS HENEAGE

## 55. 'Idle or else but seldom busied best'

Idle or else but seldom busied best,
In court, my Lord, we lead the vainest life,
Where hopes with fears, where joys with sorrows rest,
But faith is rare, though fairest words be rife.

Here learn we vice and look on virtue's books;
Here fine deceit we hold for courtly skill.
Our care is here to wait on words and looks
And greatest work to follow others' will.

Here scorn a grace, and pride, is present thought,
Malice but might, and foulest shifts no shame,
Lust but delight, and plainest dealing nought
Where flatt'ry likes and truth bears oftest blame.

      Yet is the cause not in the place, I find,
      But all the fault is in the faulty mind.

## SIR HENRY LEE

# 56. Sir Henry Lee's Farewell to the Court

His golden locks time hath to silver turn'd
(O time too swift, O swiftness never ceasing);
His youth 'gainst time and age hath ever spurn'd,
But spurn'd in vain: youth waneth by increasing.
    Beauty, strength, youth are flowers but fading seen;    5
    Duty, faith, love are roots and ever green.

His helmet now shall make a hive for bees,
And lover's sonnets turn to holy psalms;
A man-at-arms must now serve on his knees,
And feed on prayers, which are age's alms.    10
    But though from court to cottage he depart,
    His saint is sure of his unspotted heart.

And when he saddest sits in homely cell,
He'll teach his swains this carol for a song:
'Blest be the hearts that wish my sov'reign well,    15
Curs'd be the souls that think her any wrong.'
    Goddess, allow this aged man his right,
    To be your beadsman now that was your knight.

## 57. 'Time's eldest son, Old Age, the heir of Ease'

Time's eldest son, Old Age, the heir of Ease,
Strength's foe, Love's woe, and foster to Devotion,
Bids gallant youths in martial prowess please;
As for himself, he hath no earthly motion,
But thinks sighs, tears, vows, pray'rs and sacrifices   5
As good as shows, masks, jousts or tilt devices.

Then sit thee down and say thy *Nunc dimittis*,
With *De profundis*, *Credo* and *Te Deum*,
Chant *Miserere*, for what now so fit is
As that, or this: *Paratum est cor meum*?   10
O that thy saint would take in worth thy heart,
Thou canst not please her with a better part.

When others sing *Venite exultemus*,
Stand by and turn to *Noli emulari*,
For *Quare fremuerunt* use *Oremus*,   15
*Vivat Eliza* for an *Ave Mari*.
And teach those swains that live about thy cell
To say *Amen* when thou dost pray so well.

## 58. 'Far from triumphing court and wonted glory'

Far from triumphing court and wonted glory,
He dwelt in shady unfrequented places;
Time's prisoner now, he made his pastime story,
Gladly forgets court's erst afforded graces;
That goddess whom he serv'd to heaven is gone,     5
And he on earth in darkness left to moan.

But lo! a glorious light from his dark Rest
Shone from the place where erst this goddess dwelt,
A light whose beams the world with fruit hath bless'd.
Bless'd was the knight while he that light beheld;     10
Since then a star fix'd on his head hath shin'd,
And a saint's image in his heart is shrin'd.

Ravish'd with joy, so grac'd by such a saint,
He quite forgot his cell, and, self denied,
He thought it shame in thankfulness to faint;     15
Debts due to princes must be duly paid.
Nothing so hateful to a noble mind
As, finding kindness, for to prove unkind.

But ah, poor knight, though thus in dreams he rang'd,
Hoping to serve this saint in sort most meet,     20
Time with his golden locks to silver chang'd
Hath with age-fetters bound him hands and feet;
'Ay me!' he cries, 'Goddess, my limbs grow faint;
Though I time's prisoner, be you my saint!'

# Notes

**1. In Commendation of *The Steel Glass*:** *The Steel Glass* is a blank verse satire by George Gascoigne, published in 1576 with this poem recommending it; **l.3 stomachs:** men of touchy temper; **l.4 Deem:** think; **percase:** perhaps; **l.8 wights:** men; **l.9 nought, or light, esteem:** think nothing, or little, of; **l.13 censure:** judgement.

**2. A Farewell to False Love:** Some versions add another two stanzas, probably not by Ralegh:

> A quenchless fire, a nurse of trembling fear,
> A path that leads to peril and mishap;                               20
> A true retreat of sorrow and despair,
> An idle boy that sleeps in Pleasure's lap;
> A deep mistrust of that which certain seems,
> A hope of that which reason doubtful deems.
>
> Sith then thy trains my younger years betray'd,                     25
> And for my faith ingratitude I find,
> And sith repentance hath my wrongs bewray'd
> Whose course was ever contrary to kind,
> False love, Desire and Beauty frail, adieu;
> Dead is the root whence all these fancies grew.

**l.13 foil'd:** overthrown; **l.25 Sith:** since; **trains:** snares; **l.27 bewray'd:** made known; **l.28 kind:** nature.

**2a. 'Most welcome Love ...':** **l.5 fancy:** imagination, inclination; **l.11 conceit:** thought, fancy.

**3. An Epitaph Upon ... Sir Philip Sidney ...:** **l.2 And want thy wit:** without your intelligence and poetic power; **l.4 Nor any ... breath:** Nor does any one living have what is worth Sidney's life, death or wit; **ll.5–12 Yet rich ... hath doubled more:** Rich in zeal, care and love, which have been doubled by your death, even I ... now lament your fate; **l.11 seld:** seldom; **l.12 timeless:** eternal; **l.17 A king:** Philip II of Spain; **l.20 sort:** consort; **l.22 stayed:** held back; **ll.23–4 The fruits ... the seals of truth:** In young manhood you had the properties of wise age; what you intended you spoke; your words were the guarantors of truth; **l.39 the proud Castilians:** Sidney died at the battle of Zutphen in the Low Countries fighting for the Protestant cause against the Spanish rulers of the country; **l.43 dure:** last; **l.48 Thy friends thy want:** i.e. your friends have to do without you; **l.52 sprite:** spirit; **l.53 lib'ral:** generous; **l.57 Hannibal:** Hannibal Gonzago, Spanish nobleman, died at Zutphen; Hannibal was the enemy of Rome defeated by Scipio; **l.58 Scipio, Cicero, and Petrarch:** i.e. soldier, orator (Cicero the Roman statesman) and poet (Petrarch, poet of the Italian Renaissance).

4. **'Fortune hath taken thee away, my love':** **l.14 bands:** bonds.

4a. **'Ah, silly pug . . .':** **l.9 rede:** advice; **l.12 try:** test your mettle; **l.19 bands:** bonds.

5. **An Epigram on Henry Noel:** **l.1 the letter of fifty:** L is the Roman numeral for fifty – hence no-L.

5a. **'The foe to the stomach . . .':** i.e. raw-lie.

6. **The Excuse:** **l.1 Calling to mind . . . long about:** Remembering how my eye long went about; **l.4 By whose device:** on whose account.

7. **A Vision upon this Conceit of *The Faerie Queene*: Conceit:** conception; ***The Faerie Queene:*** allegorical romantic epic poem by Edmund Spenser, published in 1590 with this poem and the next commending it; **l.1 Laura:** celebrated by Petrarch, the admired Italian Renaissance poet, in his poems; **l.2 vestal flame:** flame tended by virgins as at the altar of Vesta in ancient Rome; **l.4 buried dust:** i.e. Laura's grave; **l.14 access:** coming; **thief:** because *The Faerie Queene* 'stole' the glory other poets thought their due.

8. **Another of the Same:** Another poem on *The Faerie Queene*; **l.2 Philumena:** the nightingale; **l.4 to whom they written been:** *The Faerie Queene* is a poem in praise of Queen Elizabeth I; **l.6 eyne:** eyes.

9. **Farewell to the Court:** **l.3 fancy . . . retir'd:** devotion withdrawn into myself; **l.14 fold:** shelter.

10. **'Now we have present made':** Presumably sung or spoken when a

gift was presented to the Queen; **ll.2–3 Cynthia ... Aurora:** Cynthia, Phoebe and Diana are all names for the virgin goddess of the moon and appropriate to a virgin queen; Flora, goddess of flowers; Aurora, of the dawn; l.22 **Affection:** good will; l.24 **deceive her:** do her injustice.

11. **'If Cynthia be a queen ...':** Another poem, obscure in expression, probably written when Ralegh had fallen into disfavour, to accompany other poems, asking that they not be made public. The Queen is here called Cynthia, after the virgin goddess of the moon; l.2 **these:** ?accompanying poems; **ll.5–7 thou ... Thy mind:** i.e. Ralegh ... Ralegh's mind.

12. **'My body in the walls captiv'd':** Written at the time of Ralegh's disgrace, probably alluding to his imprisonment in the Tower of London; l.6 **erst:** formerly.

13. **The Ocean's Love to Cynthia, Book Twenty-one:** This part of the poem and the fragment of Book Twenty-two are all that survive, if ever existed. Only one manuscript survives, and it is in Ralegh's own hand. Ralegh is symbolically the ocean because he is ruled by the Queen, whom he calls Cynthia, goddess of the moon. Probably written at the time of Ralegh's disgrace in 1592. l.3 **fancy:** inclination; **l.5 If ... my muse address'd:** Ralegh's joys are dead; he does not speak to them as a living person. There is no implication that the Queen is dead. l.12 **idea but resting:** likeness merely hanging on; l.15 **affections:** properties; l.21 **fruitful:** perhaps a mistake for 'fruitless'; l.28 **Philomen:** the nightingale; l.30 **renew ... conceit:** refresh my doleful thoughts; l.31 **fantasy:** careless desire; l.40 **transpersant:** piercing; l.41 **fancy's adamant:** drawing my love as a magnet does iron; **ll.59–60 Transferred ... thought's retreat:** Sometimes sympathized with her ambitious plans, sometimes with more private and retired thoughts; l.114 **grieve:** cause grief; l.116 **embalm'd:** anointed and soothed; l.123 **'Of all ... stays':** cf. the recurring line in poem 9; l.125 **sorrowful success:** the sorrow that was to come; l.129 **recure:** remedy; l.144 **fancy's:** love's; l.150 **stranger mind:** mind of a stranger; l.162 **apal'd:** made pale; l.174 **worlds:** with a rolled r to make two syllables; l.180 **tragedy:** downfall; l.189 **vestal:** virgin; **ll.193–200 These were ... powerful empery ...':** May be a false start; the three dots at 200 are Ralegh's and could mean that he meant to cancel these lines; l.199 **dure:** last; l.201 **want:** something lacking; **ll.205–8 And like ... heat of day:** According to Genesis 1:7 God placed waters above the firmament as well as on the earth. These lines refer to the

former; l.210 **change of fantasy:** whimsical tendency to alter; l.228 **careful:** producing trouble and pain; l.240 followed in the manuscript by two lines crossed out:

> And on those wither'd stalks no sign remaineth
> Of those incarnate beauties erst so pleasing

l.271 **Belphoebe:** a character in Spenser's *Faerie Queene* representing Elizabeth; l.278 **foil'd:** spoiled; l.295 **conceit:** favourable estimation, fancy; l.296 **dureless:** unlasting; l.308 **incarnate:** red; l.338 **forethought:** intended; l.341 **sith:** since; l.348 **idea:** pattern; l.349 **embalming:** sweetening; l.350 **after:** later; l.366 **sometime had regard:** were paid attention once; l.367 **But those ... have excus'd:** The pains she takes have made up for and made dispensable your faults and inadequacies; l.386 **joys:** enjoys; l.391 **assays:** attacks; ll.392, 406 **pearl, world's:** with a rolled r to make two syllables; l.414 **relapse:** falling into error; l.422 **External fancy ... recureth:** Time alone heals love of externals; l.432 **incarnate:** red; l.449 Followed by two lines which Ralegh crossed out:

> Though all her thoughts be drawn back to her breast
> And none remain that call thee to her

l.465 **false:** misdirected; l.469 **Could it be ... for those?:** Could anyone think that I loved you in order to be rewarded with this suffering?; l.484 **bett:** beat; ll.487–8 **On Sestus' shore ... guide her love:** Leander swam the Hellespont to visit Hero in Sestos, guided by her light; l.494 **draws weakly:** has little force; l.497 **Unfold:** Lead out of the pen; l.504 **brast:** broken; l.511 **draws:** drags.

**14. The Ocean's Love to Cynthia, Book Twenty-two:** This follows on from its predecessor in the manuscript and is left unfinished. l.7 **these:** these joys.

**15. The Lie:** 'Giving the lie' – telling someone to his face that he lied – was grounds for a duel; l.2 **arrant:** errand; l.33 **metes:** measures; l.39 **blasteth:** decays; l.61 **arts:** learning both practical and theoretical.

**15a. 'Go, echo of the mind ...':** l.12 **Samuels:** Samuel, in the Old Testament Book of Judges, is a type of the good judge; l.19 **words:** with a rolled r to make two syllables; l.25 **want a name:** suggesting that the poem was originally anonymous, though line 2 indicates that it was assumed to be Ralegh's.

16. **'Nature, that wash'd her hands in milk':** l.12 **wantonness:** high spirits.

17. **'What is our life? It is a play of passion':** I print what is most likely to be Ralegh's version. The poem is better known in a debased form:

> What is our life? A play of passion,
> Our mirth the music of division.
> Our mothers' wombs the tiring-houses be
> Where we are dress'd for this short comedy;
> Heaven the judicious sharp spectator is                5
> That sits and marks still who doth act amiss.
> Our graves that hide us from the searching sun
> Are like drawn curtains when the play is done.
>> Thus march we playing to our latest rest,
>> Only we die in earnest, that's no jest.           10

l.2 **division:** between the acts; l.3 **tiring-houses:** green-rooms.

18. **To the Translator of Lucan:** The translator of Lucan's poem about the Roman civil war, *Pharsalia*, was Ralegh's kinsman, Sir Arthur Gorges. The translation appeared in 1614 with this poem commending it; **l.7 in just and in religious wars:** Gorges was with Ralegh in the 1597 expedition to the Azores against the Spanish and was wounded at the landing at Fayal.

19. **A Petition to Queen Anne:** There is no knowing whether the petition ever reached its destination, the wife of James I. It was presumably written whilst Ralegh was in the Tower of London from 1603 to 1616. It exists in three versions, of which I give the earliest and most complete. The first six lines are from the opening of poem 14. Of the later versions the first uses lines 1–6 and 19–60, interpolating these three lines after 45:

> But mercy is fled to God that mercy made,
> Compassion dead, faith turn'd to policy,
> Which knows not those which sit in sorrow's shade.

The last version starts with lines 37–39 followed by the three lines printed above and an additional three:

> For what we sometime were we are no more.
> Fortune hath chang'd our shape, and destiny
> Defac'd the very form we had before.

There follow lines 40–42, then:

> But kings call not to mind what vassals were
> But know them now as envy hath describ'd them;
> So can I look on no side from despair.

Lines 46–54 and 67–78 end the draft. Both later drafts show some verbal variation on the original version.
**l.42 suspected:** imagined; **l.50 her:** Queen Anne; **l.53 Brittannies:** the two kingdoms of Britain, Scotland and England, brought together by James I; **l.77 her we had:** Elizabeth I.

20. **'My broken pipes shall on the willow hang':** A fragment; **l.2 Like those:** See Psalms 137:1.

21. **'Ev'n such is time, which takes in trust':** The last stanza of poem 16 varied and with an additional couplet. Most likely candidate for the poem written by Ralegh the night before his execution in 1618.

22. **Verse Translations from *The History of the World*:** These snippets translate quotations in Ralegh's *History of the World* and were never intended to stand alone. **i.** Two elegies on the death of Maecenas, Horace's patron, survive and were ascribed in Ralegh's time, but not in ours, to Albinovanus Pedo, poet and wit. **ii.** Supposed to be spoken by a picture of Dido, whose story is told in Vergil's *Aeneid*. He is here accused of lying. The poem (Epigram 118 in an old numbering) is no longer attributed to Ausonius, a late Latin poet. **l.4 Maro:** Vergil. **iv. l.2 bandogs:** watchdogs. **viii.** Fragments and whole poems survive of different dates associated with the cult of Orpheus and sometimes attributed to him. They were much studied in the Renaissance for their magical and religious wisdom. **x.** The original is in prose. **xi.** Aeneas' father, Anchises, speaks of the origin of his people. **xii.** When Aeneas visits the underworld he is instructed by his father's spirit.

23–27. These poems are possibly Ralegh's; the attribution of 28 is much debated; the editor's opinion is that it may be Ralegh's in part. Attribution of the other poems in this section is highly doubtful.

23. 'Sweet are the thoughts where Hope persuadeth Hap': l.1 Hap: chance, circumstance; l.9 in mauger of: despite.

24. A Poem put into my Lady Leighton's Pocket: Lady Leighton was a married woman and lady of the Privy Chamber. The Queen was godmother to her daughter, born 1582. l.6 speed: thrive.

25. A Poesy to Prove Affection is not Love: 'Affection' here means 'passionate feeling'. l.1 Conceit: fanciful love; l.10 quails: dies.

27. Sir Walter Ralegh to his Son: l.7 bag: used as a hood for the victim.

28. The Passionate Man's Pilgrimage: l.3 scrip: pilgrim's bag; l.9 palmer: pilgrim from the Holy Land; l.25 suckets: sweetmeats; l.34 pearl: with a rolled r to make two syllables; l.42 angels: with a pun on the coin of that name.

29. 'As you came from the holy land': l.2 Walsingham: A place of pilgrimage in Norfolk in the late Middle Ages; l.32 fast: secure; l.33 dureless: unlasting.

30. The Nymph's reply to the Shepherd: l.7 Philomel: the nightingale.

32. 'Prais'd be Diana's fair and harmless light': l.1 Diana: goddess of the moon and as a virgin queen type of Elizabeth I; l.18 Circes: Circe is the witch in Homer who can turn men into beasts.

33. 'Like to a hermit poor in place obscure': l.3 recure: remedy.

34. 'Feed still thyself, thou fondling, with belief': l.6 new: renew itself (by changing its object); l.9 careful: troubled; l.13 Force thy affects ... daily chase: Make yourself continue in your feeling despite the disdain with which you are treated.

36. 'Those eyes which set my fancy on a fire': l.10 of right that wears: that rightly wears.

37. 'A secret murder hath been done of late': l.9 fear'd: mistrustful; l.12 the kind: womankind; l.14 For at your sight ... bleed anew: A corpse was said to bleed in the presence of its murderer.

39. 'What else is hell but loss of blissful heaven': l.3 **beriv'n:** bereft.

40. On the Cards and the Dice: l.1 **sixth day:** of January, i.e. Twelfth Night, the last day of Christmas festivities such as the gaming of this poem; l.5 **crosses:** coins so marked; l.15 **An herald strange:** a cockerel sounding the end of the Christmas period.

42. 'A hapless kind of life is this I wear': l.4 **assays:** trials.

42a. 'Madam, but mark the labours of our life': l.5 **travail:** labour.

43. 'The doubt of future foes exiles my present joy': l.10 **wights:** men; l.16 **gape:** hope.

44. On Monsieur's Departure: 'Monsieur' is the Duke of Anjou who unsuccessfully sought the hand of Elizabeth in marriage in 1581.

45. 'Now leave and let me rest': This poem is not certainly Elizabeth's.

46. 'Seated between the old world and the new': l.7 **Supplying:** making up for; l.12 **policy:** craft.

48. 'To plead my faith where faith hath no reward': l.11 **mischief:** misfortune; l.13 **fond:** foolish.

49. 'Happy were he could finish forth his fate': l.10 **robin:** Essex was known as Robin.

50. Verses Made by the Earl of Essex in his Trouble: l.12 **get the liberty:** get free of my love.

52. 'I am not as I seem to be': l.10 **Pompey:** Caesar's rival in the Roman civil war; l.28 **prefix it:** predetermine its outcome.

53. 'The lively lark stretch'd forth her wing': l.5 **Aurora:** goddess of the dawn; l.6 **Descried:** perceived; **Thetis' bed:** There is confusion here. Aurora's bed is the guilty one, since she sleeps with a mortal, Tithonus, who grows shamefully old. Thetis is the respectable sea-nymph mother of Achilles.

**54. 'When wert thou born, Desire?'** l.4 **Good Conceit:** Favourable Impression; l.22 **Favour:** Beautiful Countenance.

**55. 'Idle or else but seldom busied best':** l.9 **present thought:** the thought of the moment.

**56. Farewell to the Court:** This used to be attributed to George Peele. It was written for Lee's retirement at the age of 57 from the office of Elizabeth's champion at the Accession Day Tilt in 1590. l.12 **His saint:** Elizabeth.

**57. 'Time's eldest son, Old Age, the heir of Ease':** l.2 **foster:** foster-child; l.4 **motion:** inclination; l.7 *Nunc dimittis*: the prayer beginning 'Lord now lettest thou thy servant depart'; l.8 *De profundis*: Psalms 130:1 'Out of the depths have I cried unto thee, O Lord'; *Te Deum*: hymn of thanks and praise; l.9 *Miserere*: have pity; l.10 *Paratum ... meum*: My heart is prepared; l.13 *Venite exultemus*: Come let us rejoice; l.14 *Noli emulari*: Psalms 37:1 'Fret not thyself because of evildoers'; l.15 *Quare fremuerunt*: Psalms 2:1 'Why do the heathen rage?'; *Oremus*: Let us pray; l.16 *Vivat Eliza*: Long live Elizabeth; *Ave Mari*: Hail Mary.

**58. 'Far from triumphing court and wonted glory':** Not strictly an Elizabethan poem, but written on the occasion of a visit in 1608 to Lee at his home near Woodstock, Lee's Little Rest, by James's consort, Queen Anne; l.3 **story:** history.

# Index of First Lines

A hapless kind of life is this I wear   77
A secret murder hath been done of late   70
Ah, silly pug, wert thou so sore afraid?   9
As you came from the holy land   60
Before the sixth day of the next new year   73
Calling to mind mine eye went long about   11
Change thy mind since she doth change   83
Come live with me and be my love   62
Conceit begotten by the eyes   55
Cowards fear to die, but courage stout   74
Ev'n such is time, which takes in trust   45
Far from triumphing court and wonted glory   94
Farewell, false Love, thou oracle of lies   4
Feed still thyself, thou fondling, with belief   67
Fortune hath taken thee away, my love   8
Give me my scallop shell of quiet   58
Go soul, the body's guest   34
Go, echo of the mind, a careless truth protest   37
Had Lucan hid the truth to please the time   40
Happy were he could finish forth his fate   85
His golden locks time hath to silver turn'd   92
I am not as I seem to be   88
I am not as I seem, I seem and am the same   87
I am that Dido which thou here dost see   46
I grieve, and dare not show my discontent   79
Idle or else but seldom busied best   91
If all the world and love were young   63
If Cynthia be a queen, a princess and supreme   16
In the main sea the isle of Crete doth lie   48
Lady, farewell, whom I in silence serve   54
Like to a hermit poor in place obscure   66
Like truthless dreams, so are my joys expir'd   14
Madam, but mark the labours of our life   77
Many by valour have deserv'd renown   47

# INDEX OF FIRST LINES

Many desire, but few or none deserve   64
Methought I saw the grave where Laura lay   12
Most welcome Love, thou mortal foe to lies   5
My body in the walls captiv'd   17
My broken pipes shall on the willow hang   44
My day's delight, my spring-time joys foredone   41
My days' delights, my spring-time joys fordone   33
My first-born love, unhappily conceiv'd   68
Nature, that wash'd her hands in milk   38
Now leave and let me rest   80
Now we have present made   15
One fire than other burns more forcibly   48
Passions are liken'd best to floods and streams   56
Prais'd be Diana's fair and harmless light   65
Seated between the old world and the new   82
Sought by the world, and hath the world disdain'd   71
Sufficeth it to you, my joys interr'd   18
Sweet are the thoughts where Hope persuadeth Hap   53
Sweet were the sauce would please each kind of taste   3
Th'Egyptians think it sin to root up or to bite   47
The brazen tower, with doors close barr'd   47
The doubt of future foes exiles my present joy   78
The first of all is God, and the same last is he   48
The foe to the stomach and the word of disgrace   10
The heaven and earth and all the liquid main   49
The lively lark stretch'd forth her wing   89
The moisten'd osier of the hoary willow   47
The plants and trees, made poor and old   46
The praise of meaner wits this work like profit brings   13
The sun may set and rise   46
The ways on earth have paths and turnings known   86
The word of denial and the letter of fifty   10
Then, marking this my sacred speech, but truly lend   48
Those eyes which set my fancy on a fire   69
Three things there be that prosper all apace   57
Time's eldest son, Old Age, the heir of Ease   93
To plead my faith where faith hath no reward   84
To praise thy life or wail thy worthy death   6
What else is hell but loss of blissful heaven   72
What is our life? It is a play of passion   39
When wert thou born, Desire   90

# Acknowledgements

This book would not have been possible without the labour of many scholars before me. I should like in particular to mention the work of Professor Michael Rudick, whose Ph.D. thesis for the University of Chicago was the best account of Ralegh's poems available until the publication of his Renaissance English Texts Society edition in 1999, and Professor Steven W. May whose books on *Sir Walter Ralegh* (Boston, Mass., 1989) and *The Elizabethan Courtier Poets* (Columbia, Missouri, 1991) are indispensable guides for the student. I have also profited greatly from the work of Pierre Lefranc, Leicester Bradner, Thomas Clayton, Philip Edwards and my late former colleague in the University of London, Agnes C. Latham. My grateful thanks also go to Professor Katherine Duncan-Jones, my computer-wise colleague Noel Heather and the staff of the library at Royal Holloway, University of London, especially the master-magician David Ward. All errors, however, may be safely ascribed to the editor, myself.

MARTIN DODSWORTH